C Here

Introduction to Programming with C

in

Linux

and on

Raspberry Pi

By Andrew Johnson

Table of Contents

Dedication

This guide is dedicated to all those who have made its production possible – from people in my own family to teachers, tutors and mentors that have guided and instructed me over the years. Also, we should all be thankful to many selfless and devoted developers, engineers and "geeks" who have helped realise the software technologies which play such a large role in our lives in this, the so-called 21st century...

Author Biography

Andrew Johnson grew up in Yorkshire, England and graduated from Lancaster University in 1986 with a degree in Computer Science and Physics. Following this, he mainly worked in Software Engineering for about 20 years, in the fields of telecommunications, process control and embedded systems. He has also worked full and part time in lecturing and tutoring and assessing (in Adult Education).

Since 2012, he has followed Raspberry Pi developments and worked on 2 small personal Pi projects – an aircraft tracker and a simple Python-Based media kiosk project.

In his spare time, he has widely researched a number of "alternative knowledge" topics which he has written on his website - www.checktheevidence.com. He can be contacted via that site or through ad.johnson2211@gmail.com.

Chapter 1 - Introduction

This guide attempts to introduce the 'C' Programming Language to the novice programmer. Some readers will perhaps be more familiar with Java, Javascript, PHP or even C# - all of which have a number of keyword and syntactic features which seem to have been borrowed or derived from C. (As an aside, it is highly likely that compilers and interpreters for these languages were originally written in C or C++.)

You should find the examples easy to digest and when I originally delivered what is in this guide as a 10-week evening class (i.e. about 20 hours of study and practice), it seemed to be well-received and helped a number of people learn programming for the first time, although C is not normally considered a beginner's programming language.

This guide will <u>not</u> teach you everything you need to know about C programming, nor programming in general. Neither will it teach you everything you need to know about Linux or Raspberry Pi's. It is almost entirely devoted to teaching you the **fundamentals of the C language, using Linux and/or Raspberry Pi as a platform for doing this.** The guide does not go into the more advanced features of the C language, nor does it discuss system programming much, if at all. It does, however, discuss the use of pointers in C.

A companion guide **Advanced C Programming** should be available by the time you read this. (This will cover the use of C Structures, more advanced pointer usage, bit and byte level access, binary file access and topics such as dynamic memory allocation.)

1.1 Introduction to 'C'

The 'C' Language "rose to fame" in the 1980's, having been used in the smallest microprocessor systems to the largest mainframes and supercomputers. The language's popularity probably stems from its flexibility and its ease of access to low-level features which can give a great deal of control over the host system.

It is rather a strange language and can be very cryptic (have a look at this example - http://bit.ly/2qAkPVH), perhaps because it can still maintain some of its original low-level appearance. For the inexperienced programmer, there are many pitfalls - some of which this guide attempts to highlight. Once mastered, however, the 'C' language offers a suitable compromise between a high and low level language. Since the turn of the millennium, C has arguably undergone something of a "comeback," with the increasing uptake and usage of Linux across many computing platforms and the widespread availability of advanced free open source C compilers and associated development environments, one of which ("Codeblocks") we will use in this guide.

For the potential C++ programmer, learning the original C language is probably not a bad idea, as most of the fundamentals of C++ are the same as those for C.

Applications of C

It is used by professionals and hobbyists. It is a general purpose language - used in the development of Microprocessor Software, Device Drivers, early Operating Systems, Applications Software and Games! It is most commonly used through a compiler, although at least one C interpreter (Ch) has become available in recent years.

Serious and continued use of C in programming will force you to learn more about the underlying nature of the computer and the operating system you are using. Using C, you are often forced to think at a "lower machine level" when writing programs. In more modern programming languages, much of the low-level activity is hidden away in runtime libraries or "imported modules". With C, you are at the "bleeding edge" of the system, in most cases.

1.2 History of 'C'

The UNIX operating system was developed in parallel with the C programming language. Now, of course, Linux has been developed to be a working clone of UNIX, hence C can essentially be considered a "native" programming language for Linux.

'C' had its beginnings in a language called BCPL, which was introduced in the 1960's. From this, a language called 'B' was developed and this subsequently became 'C,' written by Dennis Kernighan at Bell Labs in 1972. Later in the 1970's 'C' became more widely used and an important milestone in the language's history was in 1978 when Brian Kernighan and Dennis Ritchie published a 'C' Language Reference Manual. This eventually became the recognised standard for the language, but was not official.

By 1988, the language was being so widely used that ANSI produced a standard for the language - largely based on Kernighan and Ritchie's 2nd edition of the reference manual. All 'C' compilers which are said to be ANSI compliant adhere to the standards laid down by ANSI in 1988.

1.3 Philosophy of 'C'

The 'C' philosophy is always *"the programmer knows what he / she is doing"*, and there are few safeguards for the careless programmer. The language's attitude is much different than BASIC or some of the sophisticated newer languages such as Java, Python and C#. It allows you to write illegal and nonsensical code. Its syntax and type checking are weak, though default settings in modern compilers enforce more strict programming options. The main advantage of C is that you have a great deal of flexibility and, for instance, access to machine hardware is often trivially simple compared to other languages. Also, 'C' compilers can generate compact and well-optimised code which is ideal for small scale applications, but also useful for larger ones where you just need "that bit more" from your system. Time critical applications can often still benefit from being coded in C, not just because compiled code can run hundreds of times faster than interpreted code, but also because C programs can often "bypass" certain operating system features which compromise the performance of a program/application.

Chapter 2 - Using This Guide

1) You will need to have a device capable of running a version of Linux that dates from approximately 2012 onwards. I will be referring to Ubuntu and Raspbian versions of Linux, which are both derivatives of Debian.

2) You need know how to be able to use commands in a terminal window or through a command line in Linux and/or install a Linux Application using the Software Centre (Ubuntu), App Grid or some other GUI or command line based application installer such "apt-get".

2.1 Using Windows or Mac Systems for Learning C

If you don't have Linux and don't want to install it on your computer, you can still use Linux and C fairly easily, providing you have plenty of Disk Space. Just search for "Installing **Virtual Box**" and "Ubuntu Linux and Virtual Box." If you can successfully install these on your Windows or Mac Computer, you can still use the instructions in Section Chapter 5 - and the rest of this guide to get you going. You will need approximately 20GB of space to install everything. To use VirtualBox successfully, you may need to change a "Virtualisation" setting in your BIOS. Research online for further details.

2.2 Be Aware!

Linux is updated almost daily – with the result that features in applications software get moved around, deleted and/or changed. Graphics get re-designed and applications become superseded or outdated.

This means that instructions given in section Chapter 5 - may not be quite up to date when you read them, or the results they give might be slightly different. You may therefore need to experiment a bit and also search online for updated instructions or notes about new features and enhancements or changes.

You have been warned! ☺

2.3 Rationale of Examples

Some of the example programs may seem pointless or unrealistic - in such cases, they are written to illustrate features of the language rather than being useful programs in their own right.

You can of course download all the sample programs and compile and run them, but you may find you will learn the language better if you actually type them (as was more common place when this guide was originally created in the early 1990's). If you type and compile the programs yourself, you will learn more about what the error messages mean and you will get better at spotting errors in your code, when you start to write some!

2.4 Course Theme

When I originally began programming, back in 1981 on a Sinclair ZX81, I was motivated to write a simple game. A similar thing happened a year later when I got the legendary Spectrum (16K model). In this guide, then, we will adopt a similar "plan". We will be building up our knowledge to write a simple "code cracking" game – known to many as "Mastermind".

Code Cracking Game – "Mastermind"

This is a game I used to enjoy playing as a child – I even had a pocket electronic version. A sequence of digits (in the range 0 – 9) is set as a "secret code" (it is normally set by a human – the code setter, but we'll get the computer to do it). The "code breaker" then tries to guess the code as quickly as possible. He or she makes guesses by placing them on a board – typically, the user has 10 attempts at guessing the code before the game is over. The "code setter" then "marks" the guess according to certain rules:-

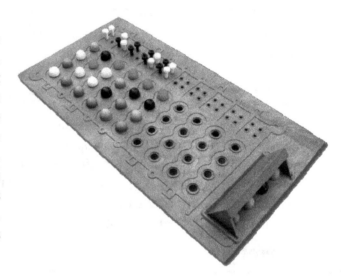

- If, in the guess, there is a certain number which is also in the code, but it is in a **DIFFERENT** position, a **WHITE** peg is awarded.

- If, in the guess, there is a certain number which is also in the code, but it is in the **SAME** position, a **BLACK** peg is awarded.

- Only 1 white or black peg per correct digit is awarded.

Example

- If the secret code was "1234" and the guess was "4255", one black peg (for the "2") and one white peg (for the "4") would be awarded.

- In the example shown below (grabbed from the working version of the program we will develop), there is either a 3 or 4 in the code, and the secret code does *not* end in a 4, may have a 3 in it, but if it does have a 3 in it, it's not in the first 3 positions.

Rationale

By developing an easily understandable game, which is actually quite good fun, we will be able to introduce fundamental programming concepts such as input and output, data storage (in arrays), counting, conditional tests and looping (also called iteration).

A complete listing is provided in Appendix 1.

This is what our finished, running game will look like.

2.5 Simple Programming Exercises

Appendix 2 lists some very simple ideas for programs that you can write – based on the examples given in the guide. No solutions are given.

2.6 Other Languages

If you can master what is in this guide and you understand what you have done, you will have a solid basis for developing an understanding the concepts involved in the most commonly used methods in what is called procedural computer programming. A logical next step then would be to develop an understanding of object-oriented computer programming, which is used inherently and throughout more modern programming languages such as C++, Java, Python and even in variants of BASIC.

Chapter 3 - The Programming Process – A Quick Summary

Some people would call this "algorithm development" or "algorithm design" or even "systems thinking". For the purposes of this guide, I will call it "the programming process". Whole books are available which go into minute detail about these concepts. Here, we present the essential fundamentals.

The Programming Process involves

- Considering a problem.
- Breaking up the problem into small pieces.
- Considering how to express the solution to each part of the problem in the form of a Computer Program.

A Program

Can be split into 2 main parts:-

- Instructions - Code
- Information - Data

In solving the problem, we have to consider what Information and Instructions are required.

3.1 Instructions/Code in a Program

Can be categorised into 3 main types:-

1. Information (Data) Manipulation.
2. Conditional Test.
3. Jump/Branch.

You will see different examples of each of these types on instructions in this guide, although the Jump/Branch is often done implicitly, by structuring the program in a certain way.

3.2 Information/Data in a Program

Can take many different forms. e.g.

- Simple whole number values
- Floating point values (with a decimal point)
- Text / Strings / Characters
- Graphics
- Sound

'C' is just another programming language and it has its own particular way of expressing Code & Data.

3.3 Compiled Languages

- Once a program has been written, it has to be *Compiled ("converted")* before being run. If an error is seen, the program has to be, terminated, corrected, re-compiled and run from the beginning.
- The conversion process in only done once, unless changes are made to the program.

3.4 Interpreted Languages

- Once a program has been written, it can be run straight away. If an error occurs, the program may stop completely or just stop temporarily, following an "alert" message of some kind. The program can be interrupted, corrected and the program can continue running from the point it was stopped at.

- The "conversion" process happens every time the program runs - this slows things down, although early in the 21st century, computer processors (CPU's) are often thousands of times faster than they were near the end of the 20th century.

3.5 Hybrid Languages

Some more modern languages use a combination of compilation and interpreting which can provide certain advantages in some situations.

3.6 How do we enter a 'C' program into a Computer?

To write a 'C' program we need to be able to enter and store text in the computer. To do this we use a *Text Editor.*

A Text Editor
Is a program which we run on the computer that allows us to enter, modify and save some text to disk. This text can be anything - a letter, a book, a load of rubbish, or a 'C' program.

A Compiler
Is a program which we run on a computer which converts some text into an "object code". This is code that will run on the system you have written the code for (called "the target system".) There is also another program called a "linker" which adds other "standard" code to the object code to create an "executable program."

A compiler and a text editor maybe entirely separate, but we shall be using **Codeblocks IDE** (Integrated Development Environment), where they can be considered one and the same thing.

Target System
Here, our target system is either a Raspberry Pi or Windows PC – but you can compile code on a PC or a Raspberry Pi that runs on a different type of system. This is commonly done with what are called **embedded systems**. For this sort of development, you use a cross-compiler.

3.7 What is Compilation?

- It is the process of converting a body of text into "object code" which in turn is converted into a "runnable" or **executable** program.

- The compiler checks the text against the rules for the language in question (in our case the 'C' Language) to see if it forms a valid set of instructions.

- Where the compiler finds that the rules for the language have been broken, it displays a message:-

```
"Error X line Y:     ... Description  ..."
```

or, less severe is:-

```
"Warning X line Z :    ... Description ..."
```

3.8 Edit → Compile → Link

There are actually 3 distinct stages to producing a working 'C' program they are:-

Editing	The program is entered into the computer using a text editor. The text that is entered is called *source code* or just *the source*.
Compilation	The program is converted into "object" code, similar to machine code.
Link	A program called the linker combines the object code for your program with "run time library" object code to make your program a fully working "stand alone" unit which can be run independently of the editor, linker and compiler.

Often, these stages are hidden from the user – particularly if you use an Integrated Development Environment – IDE, such as is mentioned in Section Chapter 4 - . Nowadays, "compilation" and "linking" are typically done in one step, as shown in Section Chapter 5 - .

Chapter 4 - More about Our Project

4.1 Requirements

As mentioned above, we will be building a simple game, based on the idea of "Mastermind." To do this, then, we have a problem to solve – which we will break down into the following parts (some would call the column on the left "User Requirements" or "Functional Requirements").

Code / Instructions needed to…	Data Needed
Drawing the Board	Simple Board Layout
Read in a code guess	Number in the guess
Generate a secret code	Number in the secret code
Check the code and guess	Compare "guess storage" and "secret code storage"
Display Marks for each guess	
Count guesses as we play	A single number/counter (the guess counter)
Check whether we have had too many guesses	The Guess counter
Display "Game Won" or Lost	
Restart the Game	

4.2 Flow Chart

We can re-consider this as set of steps in a flow chart, which we can then structure.

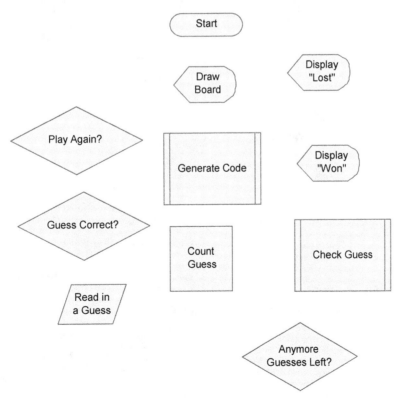

Elements of Flowchart, Unstructured.

We now consider the steps required to play the game and re-structure the flowchart, thus:

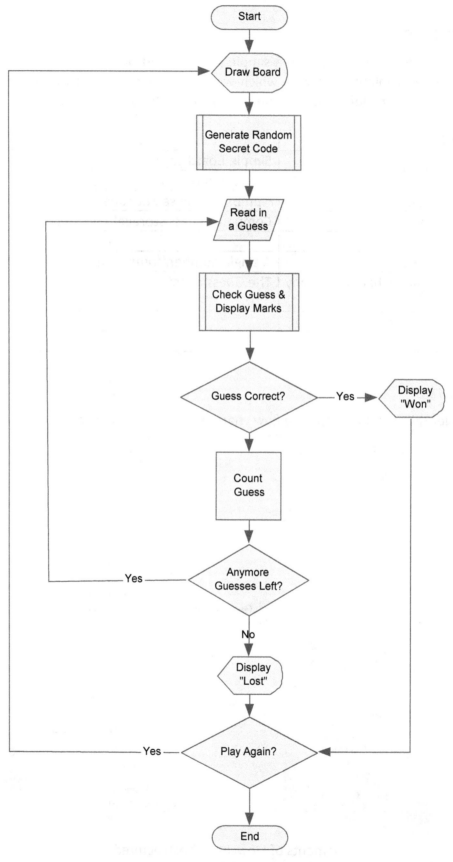

Chapter 5 - Compiling and Running C Programs

5.1 Command Line and GUI

In modern desktop operating systems, there are essentially 2 modes of user interaction:

- Graphical User Interface (a *long* time ago this was called WIMP – Window Icon Mouse Pointer!)
- Command Line or "Terminal" (The latter being a reference to how early computers provided real-time access to a computer via a Visual Display Unit – VDU – which was simply a keyboard and a screen.)

Some people prefer one method over another – though the GUI method has many advantages. If you are running a "stripped down" version of Linux – for example to run in a lower power device where you can't attach a screen, command line may be the only available method.

GUI

Here, you are simply using another application/package to compile and run programs – which operates in a very similar manner to your word processor, spreadsheet etc. You type in the program and essentially run it straight away, then go back to typing/editing.

Command Line

Here you type commands (covered in the next section) to compile and run the program and then typically type another command to run and editor program (such as "nano"). This is covered in section 5.5.

5.2 Installing Codeblocks IDE on Raspberry Pi / Linux

There are many useful and wonderful editors and IDE's available under the Linux Operating system and probably nearly as many of these are available on the Raspberry Pi. However, I have chosen the excellent "Codeblocks" IDE for this guide.

On Linux, it could be installed on your system by opening the Software Centre and searching for "Codeblocks," although this may not give you the very latest version available. However, completing the following steps will work best.

```
sudo apt-get install
```

Raspbian Jessie – Codeblocks installation from Command Line

An icon should be added to the launcher or applications folder which looks like this:

On the Raspberry Pi, once installed, Codeblocks should appear in the Applications/Programming menu:

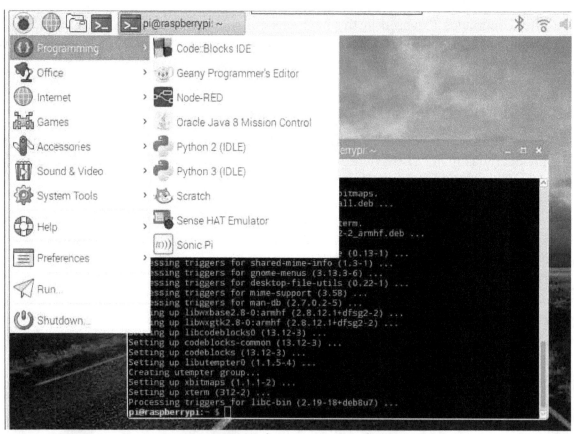

Programming Sub Menu on Raspberry Pi

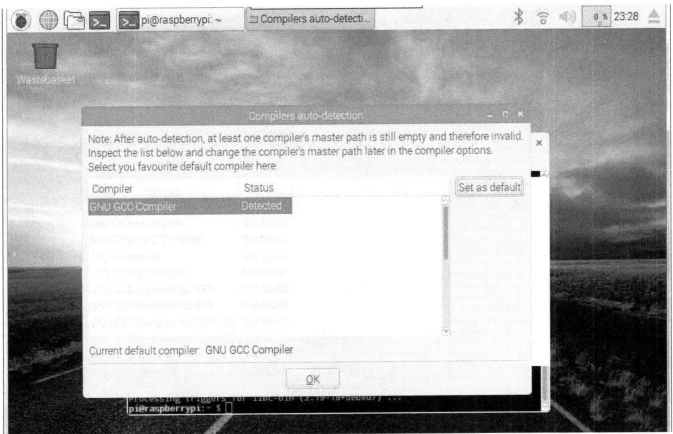

Codeblocks Compiler Detection – Should be set to gcc

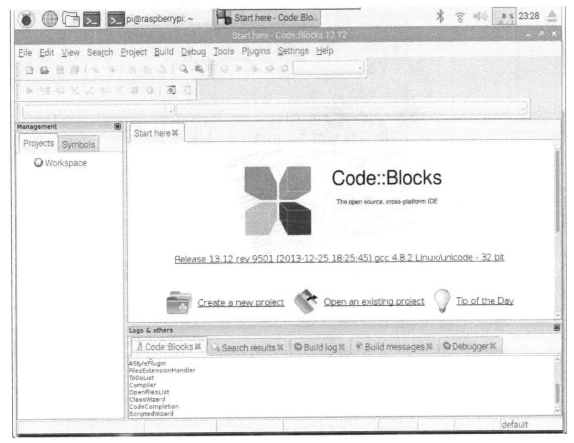

Codeblocks – Successfully Loaded and Running – Ready for a Program!

5.3 First Program – Codeblocks

There are 2 ways of getting your first program to run, both of which are outlined below.

Quick/Direct Method

1. Select "File/New" and "Create Empty File":

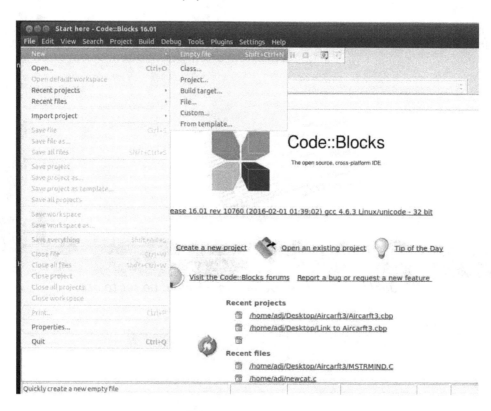

2. When you see the empty file appear, enter The following text *exactly* as shown. **Don't miss out any of the characters and take care with the quotation marks, brackets and semi-colons!**

```
/* The first 'C' program! */
#include "stdio.h"
int main( )
{
  printf ("Greetings, pop pickers!");
  getchar( );
}
```

3. Then click the "Play" button, which should give you the display shown below.

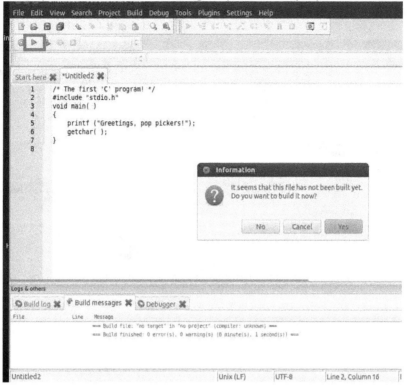

4. Click "Yes" and you should then see the display below:

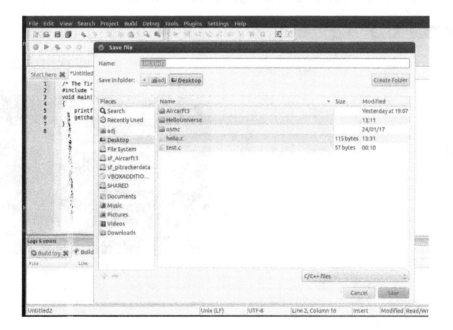

5. Type "**hello.c**" (the .c is very important here!), then click "Save"

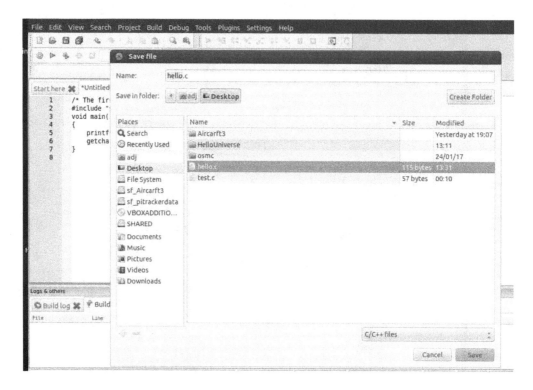

6. You should then see the display below, after a few seconds.

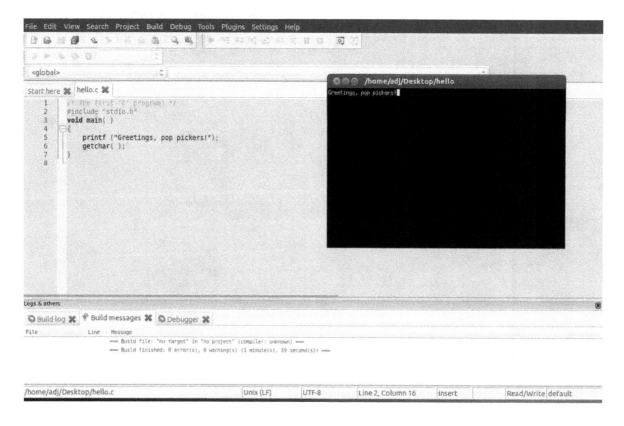

7. As you can see, the output of your program is shown in the smaller window with the black background. Press Enter twice to close this window.

Wizard Method

1. Select "File Menu" and "New" and "Project" to start a new project. Select "Console Application" and Click "Go".

2. You will be presented with some explanatory text so click "Next".

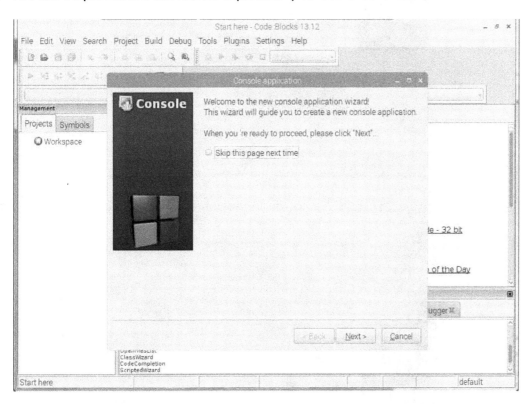

3. It asks you which Language you want to create your application in – "C" should be selected already – so click **Next**

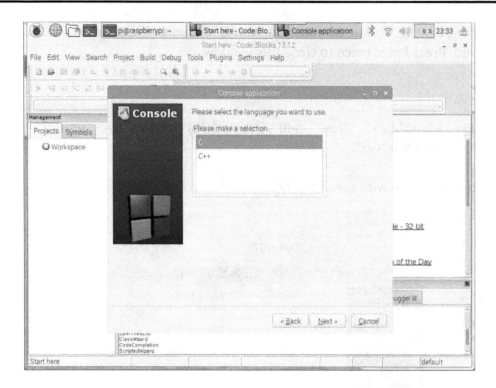

4. Type a name for your project such as "Hello" or "HelloUniverse" (thing big!) and click **Next**.

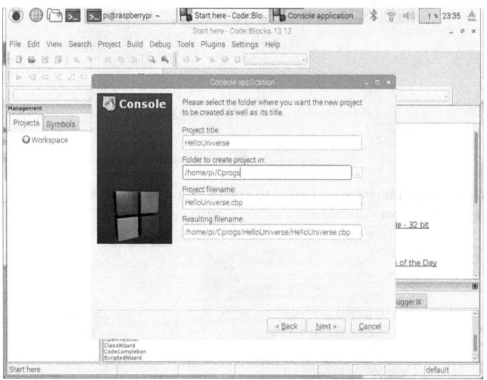

5. You will then be presented with a list of settings. Leave these settings as given and just click **Finish**.

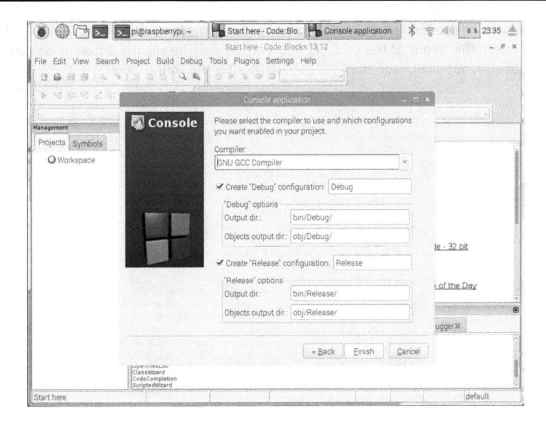

6. You should see the display shown below – so click "**main.c**" in the "Projects" panel on the left.

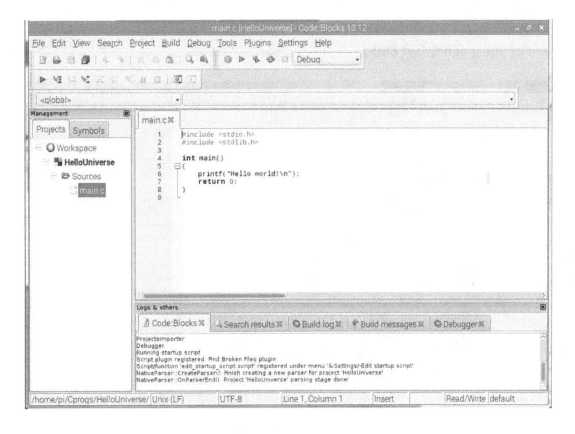

7. Codeblocks has generated a simple "Hello World" program. Feel free to change "World" to "Universe". The layout of the toolbars and buttons may be slightly different on your version. You can also, optionally, add the line "**getchar()**" after the "printf" line:

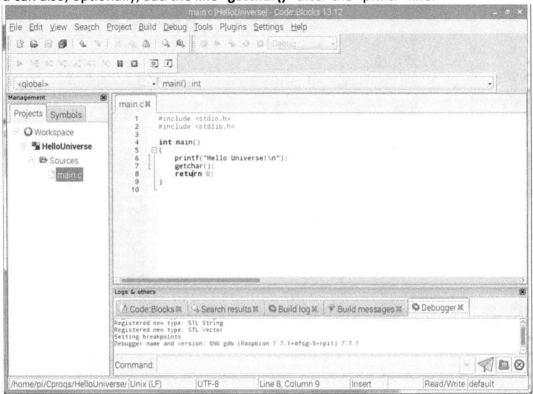

8. Now click the green "play" button on the toolbar:

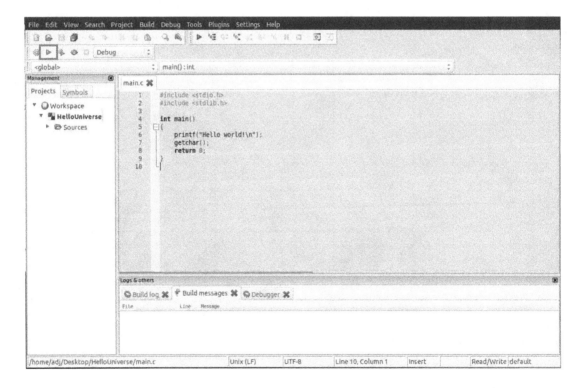

9. You should see the following display:

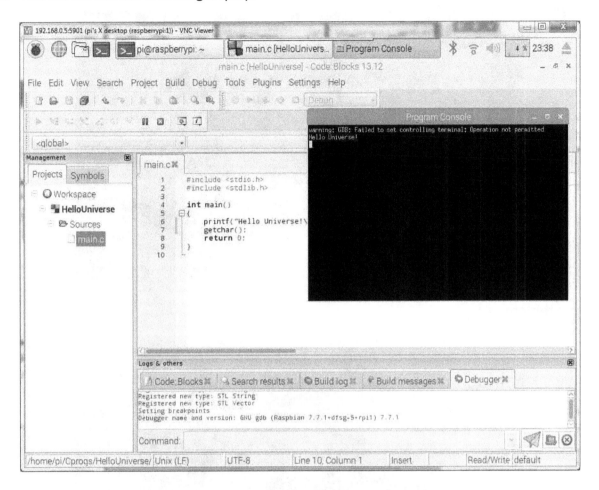

10. You can type some characters, then press Enter TWICE and the small black window will disappear. Now you can proceed to section 5.5.

5.4 First Program - Command Line Method

If you are booted into command line, you can ignore the next step.

1. Look for the "terminal" icon in the menus and click on it. Type

```
nano hello.c
```

and press Enter

2. You should see this display

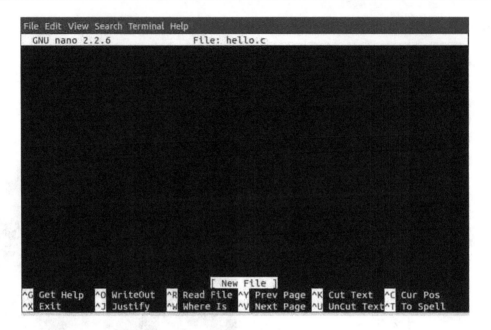

3. Type in this program

```
File Edit View Search Terminal Help
  GNU nano 2.2.6                 File: hello.c                        Modified

/* The first 'C' program! */
#include "stdio.h"
void main( )
{
        printf ("Greetings, pop pickers!");
        getchar( );
}




^G Get Help  ^O WriteOut  ^R Read File ^Y Prev Page ^K Cut Text  ^C Cur Pos
^X Exit      ^J Justify   ^W Where Is  ^V Next Page ^U UnCut Text^T To Spell
```

4. press Ctrl-X followed by "Y"

5. Type the line below and press enter

```
gcc hello.c -o hello
```

6. If you see any error messages, or get anything other than just the command prompt, you will need to check your program by typing "**nano hello.c**" again and comparing what you typed with what is shown above. Make sure it is **exactly** the same. If you don't see any error messages, just type

```
./hello
```

7. You should see the display below.

8. Press Enter to return to the command line.
9. Congratulations! You have now completed your first program and successfully run it!

5.5 The First Program - What Does This Do?

All the program does is print a message on the screen, and waits for the enter key to be pressed. Further details are given below:

1. "**main( )**" - denotes the start of the program.
2. "**{**" (open brace) means start of a "block".
3. "**printf**" is a printing "function" - output.
4. "**getchar( )**" is a keyboard reading "function" – reading a character input and wait for the Enter Key to be pressed.
5. "**}**" (close brace) means end of a block.
6. **"/* */" means "comment". The text between the "markers" is ignored by the compiler – the text is used to document the action of each step.**

By the end of this guide, you should be able understand what all the lines of the program do.

5.6 First Program – Observations

We see from this first program that:-

- 'C' is "free format" - no line numbers are typed as part of the program (some text editors will show line numbers in the left margin).
- 'C' is "block structured" - everything is specified in "blocks" between braces - { }).

> **We should also note that C is case-sensitive. This means that if you used "Printf" (with a capital "P") instead of "printf" the program *would not work*.**

In the examples which follow, the entire program is not always listed. Unless otherwise stated, you should always type programs into the following "skeleton":-

```
int main ( )
{
        <lines for your program>
}
```

5.7 A Note about "Console Applications" and The Console Window

The program we just entered, like all the others we will be looking at in this guide, runs in the **Console Window**. The **Console Window** is essentially a "throw back" to the very early days of interactive computing – where you had a basic Computer Console, which could only display characters or very limited graphics. There was no graphical user interface and very few, if any, actual graphics. If you progress to the Advanced C Programming Guide, we will look at some basic Linux Graphics features, but not GUI programming. Full GUI programming is often best understood in tandem with using Object Oriented Programming languages such as C++.

Chapter 6 - Different Types Of Data In 'C'

6.1 What is Data in a program?

It is the information required by the program to perform its function. e.g. the names and addresses of employees in a company's personnel records, the titles and artists of records in someone's collection.

Data in the real world has infinite variety. In 'C', like other programming languages, there are only certain ways to express data.

6.2 Using Data In a 'C' Program

To use data in a program, we have to **declare** it, by putting in a special line e.g.

```
int   number_of_items;
```

to declare a piece of data - an integer, a "whole number", to store the number of items for some kind of counting operation. *Code has to know what data it will be using, hence:-*

Data declarations always come before code.

Notes on Data Declaration

The data declaration shown is in 3 parts:-

```
int       number_of_items   ;
(1)             (2)        (3)
```

They are

1. Data type
2. Name for data item
3. Terminator

We call the data items we declare *variables*. The "Name" is often referred to as an *identifier*.

Names for Data Items (variables)

The naming of variables follows certain rules:-

- The variable name can't start with a number.
- The variable name cannot have spaces in it (use underscore "_" instead).
- Variable names are "case sensitive".
- They cannot use any of the following characters:- $ - + % & * ! " # ? / = ( ) ^ ~ [ ] { } | \
- The names used can not be 'C' reserved words (i.e. ones that are already used by the language such as **int, char, printf** etc.

Within any program, there is a need to store different **types** data/information. This is, most commonly, numbers or text.

6.3 Basic Data Types in C

Each piece of data then, must have a <u>type.</u> In C, there are particular names for each of these types, which are explained below.

1. **int**

"int" is used to store whole number data. Because of the way 'C' works, only numbers in the range +32,767 to - 32,768 can be stored in an "int".

2. **long**

"long" is used to store larger whole numbers from +2,147,483,647 to -2,147,483,648.

Example:-

```
long   number_of_viewers;
```

3. **char**

"char" is used to store single characters e.g. `A', `z', `q'.

Example:-

```
char first_initial;
```

Programming In 'C' on Linux & Raspberry Pi - Different Types Of Data In 'C'

4. **float** or **double**

"**float**" or "**double**" is used store floating point numbers - those with decimal places such as 3.1415926.

Example:-

```
float    ft_index;
double   exchange_rate;
```

Reasons for Having Different Data Types

It is sometimes asked why it is necessary to have different data types. The reason is not to make the language complicated and awkward to use, it is to improve the efficiency with which a program can utilise system resources. All data items use up an amount of System Memory. If we were to just say "each item of data will use 50 bytes of memory", this could be very wasteful and we would exhaust our memory earlier than necessary if we only needed one byte per item for our particular program.

Also, generally speaking, items of data which are larger take longer to process, so if we choose our data item size accordingly, we can improve the execution speed of our programs.

When C was first developed, in the 1970's, computer storage (both RAM and Disk) was/were extremely expensive, so efficient use of storage was a primary concern. In 2017, most computers have vast amounts of storage and very high speed processors – so more modern programming languages are less concerned with efficient usage of storage than C is – and they provide much better data processing facilities, within the language itself (especially when processing arrays – covered later – and lists).

6.4 Initialising Data or "Variable" Values

We can give a variable a specific value when we declare it:-

```
int   current_temperature = 25;
```

This is called *initialisation.*

- 31 -

6.5 Assigning Values to Variables

In our program, we can set variables or "assign" them to particular values in a similar way to initialisation:-

```
int main( )
{
  int number_of_items;

  number_of_items = 0;
}
```

Using Data Types

A good chunk of writing a 'C' program is working out how to express the data required in terms of the types used in 'C'.

We already saw, in the first program, how to print out some text. How do we print out the values of variables?

6.6 Printing Out Variables

Consider the following program:-

```
#include "stdio.h"
int main( )
{
  int number_of_items = 0;

  printf ("No. of items = %d ", number_of_items);
  number_of_items = number_of_items + 1;
  printf ("New No. of items = %d", number_of_items);
}
```

The program produces the following result:-

```
No. of items = 0   New No of items = 1
```

Action of the Program
1. Variable "number_of_items" is set to 0.
2. Value of variable is printed out.
3. Value of variable is increased by 1.
4. New value of variable is printed out.

The "printf" command is explained in more detail in Chapter 8 - .

Chapter 7 - Expressions, Statements and Operators

These are 2 words used to describe certain parts of any programming language and it is important to understand them.

7.1 An Expression

An expression is a collection of variable names, numbers and operators which can be used together in a calculation to produce a single result e.g.

```
a + 2*b - 4*(c+d)
```

An expression normally forms the *right hand side of an assignment statement.*

7.2 A Statement

Is any complete command in a program. In 'C', a statement is terminated by a semi-colon:

```
e = a + 2*b - 4*(c+d);
```

Here, the *expression* a + 2*b - 4*(c+d) forms *part* of the whole statement. The following is also a statement

```
printf ("Crinkly Brindlewurdles...");
```

7.3 Operators

Symbol	Operation
+	Addition
-	Subtraction
*	Multiplication
/	Division
%	Modulus (remainder)

Operators are the symbols used in the language to represent the common operations done on data. There are arithmetic and other types of operators (introduced later). In all, 'C' has a rich set of operators, but the basic ones are shown in the table above. (Later we shall see **EQUALITY TESTING** uses "= =".)

7.4 Auto-Increment and Auto-Decrement

"Increment" normally means "increase by 1", "decrement" normally means "decrease by 1". Some very useful operators in 'C' are the "auto-increment" and "auto-decrement" ones.

```
++ increments by 1.
-- decrements by 1.
```

Auto-Increment

e.g. The auto-increment operator can be seen to have the following effect:

```
i = 0;
i++;           /* i now equals 1. */
```

The auto-decrement operator has the reverse effect:-

```
i = 4;
i--;           /* i now equals 3. */
```

++ and **--** can either come ***before or after*** the variable name they are being used on - the effect is slightly different. These operators can also be put almost anywhere in a C statement e.g.

```
i = 0;
j = i++;     /* Result: i = 1, j = 0 */

/* BUT */
i = 0;
j = ++i;     /* Result: i = 1, j = 1 */
```

The auto-increment and auto-decrement operators are commonly used within "for" loops (introduced later).

Summary of Auto Increment / Decrement

In other words, increment/decrement is performed *before* the operation on the variable if the operator is placed *before,* or it is performed *after* operation on the variable if the operator is placed *after.*

7.5 Some Other Operators

Similar to ++ and -- are + = and - = are

```
+=              adds on the amount specified.
-=              subtracts the amount specified.
```

e.g.

```
i = 5;
i += 10;/* Result  is now 15. */

i = 17;
i -= 10;/* Result is now 7. */

Overall, we can say that:-

i += x;  /* equivalent to i = i + x;  */
i -= x;  /* equivalent to i = i - x; */
```

Note: Operators "/=", "*=" and "%=" are also available.

Chapter 8 - Outputting To The Screen - "Printf"

We are now going to look at the "printf" function in more detail.

```
printf ("some text", <some variables>);
  (1)           (2)              (3)
```

1. function name
2. Control String
3. Variables whose values are to be printed

The simple case of "printf" is like the first example program, which just contains text to be printed and no other variables.

8.1 Printing Values stored in Variables – "Conversion" Characters

The more complicated case is where you put one or more "conversion characters" in the "Control String". Conversion characters follow the "%" symbol. One Conversion character is "%d" which means "substitute an integer variable value here". Other Conversion characters are:-

Conversion Specifier	Purpose
%ld	is used to print long data.
%c	is used to print char data.
%f	is used to print float or double number data.
%s	is used to print string data (covered later).

NOTE: You must include a variable after the control string for every conversion character you specify, otherwise unpredictable results may occur.

Example Program Using "printf"

```
#include "stdio.h"

int main( )
{
  char any_letter;
  int any_number;
  long any_long_number;
  float any_decimal_number;

  any_letter = 'z';
  any_number = 37;
  any_long_number = 1000000;
  any_decimal_number = 9.81;

  printf ("The letter is %c.\n", any_letter);
  printf ("The number is %d.\n", any_number);
  printf ("The long number is %ld.\n",       any_long_number);
  printf ("The decimal number is %f.\n", any_decimal_number);
}
```

Notes

The program does the following:-

1. Initialises a char, int, long and float var.
2. Prints out the value of each of these, in a message, followed by a "carriage return" (new line).

But what is the "\n" here?

8.2 Special Characters with "printf"

In the last program, we saw each "message" appear on a new line. This was achieved by placing another special printing character in the "control string" - which was "\n". Hence "\n" in the control string prints a "new line". All special printing characters are preceded with a "\" (backslash) some of them are listed below:-

\n	new line (Carriage return/line feed).
\t	tab (normally max 8 spaces).
\r	carriage return only.
\b	backspace.
\\	backslash character.

It is possible to freely mix "conversion" and "special printing" characters e.g. This line can be added to the previous program:-

```
printf ("The number is %d \t\t. The long number is %ld \n",
 any_number, any_long_number);
```

8.3 Codecracker Game – Printing the Board

Now that we know how to print things out, we can write a very short program to print out a simple representation of our board (we will improve this later):

```
#include "stdio.h"

int main( )
{
    /* Print out the board. */
    printf ("%s",+----+----+\n);
    printf ("%s",|    |    |\n);
    printf ("%s",|    |    |\n);
    printf ("%s",|    |    |\n);
    printf ("%s",|    |    |\n);
    printf ("%s",|    |    |\n);
    printf ("%s",|    |    |\n);
    printf ("%s",|    |    |\n);
    printf ("%s",|    |    |\n);
    printf ("%s",|    |    |\n);
    printf ("%s",|    |    |\n);
    printf ("%s",+----+----+\n);

    /* Print out a title. */
    printf (" * * *  M A S T E R M I N D  * * *");
}
```

We still have some other things to think about:

1. How will we display the guess and the marks "inside" the play/board area?
2. How will we display each guess in a position lower down the board?

Chapter 9 - Text Strings

In the same way as we can define data items for numbers and characters, we can also define data items for text, and print them out. This is done in the following program.

```
int main ( )
{
  char android_name[ ] = "Kryten";
  char android_type[ ] = "Mechanoid 2000";

  printf ("Here comes the string... \n");
  printf ("Android's name is \t%s\n", android_name);
  printf ("Android's model number is \t %s\n", android_type);
}
```

Program Notes

The program does the following:-

1. Declares 2 string variables called "android_name" and "android_type", and initialises them to the characters shown.
2. Prints out a message.
3. Prints out each string within a message, followed by a new line.

Why do String Declarations use [ ]?
This peculiarity of declaring text strings in 'C' is due to the fact that a string is actually an *Array of Characters*. Strictly speaking, when we declare a string, we should do it thus:-

```
char any_string[18] = "Zaphod Beeblebrox";
```

Here we are declaring an array of 18 characters, to store the letters of "Zaphod Beeblebrox" - which is actually only 17 letters long! The extra character is needed because 'C' identifies the end of strings of text by a character of 0 value. The Compiler puts in a 0 character for us (invisibly), before the closing quotation mark of the string. So in 'C',

All Strings are NULL (0) Terminated.

When declaring a string, using the "[ ]" is a short cut - because the 'C' Compiler can work out the length of the string, it effectively puts this number between the "[ ]" for us.

The "Zaphod Beeblebrox" string shown above could hence be shown as an *array of characters*:-

0	1	2	3	4	5	6	7	8	9	10	11	12	13	14	15	16	17
Z	a	p	h	o	d		B	e	e	b	l	e	b	r	o	x	\0

Referencing Individual Characters in a String

Because, in the last examples, we have declared an array of characters, it is possible to reference each character individually. For instance, if we wrote the following line (in a program after the string declaration):-

```
printf ("%c\n", any_string[3]);
```

we would see 'h' appear on the screen. But this is the 4th letter of "Zaphod", not the 3rd, **why**?

Using Array Elements

When referring to array elements in 'C', you must start counting from 0. In other words, the first element in any array is always numbered 0. Hence, in 'C',

> ### Array element references (indices) start at 0.

9.1 Let's Modify our "Board Printing" Program

We will now use 2 string variables and modify how we print our board.

```
#include "stdio.h"
int main( )
{
    char board_end[]      = "+----+----+\n";
    char board_middle[]  = "|    |    |\n";

    /* Print out the board. */
    printf ("%s",board_end);
    printf ("%s",board_middle);
    printf ("%s",board_middle);
    printf ("%s",board_middle);
    printf ("%s",board_middle);
    printf ("%s",board_middle);
    printf ("%s",board_middle);
    printf ("%s",board_middle);
    printf ("%s",board_middle);
    printf ("%s",board_middle);
    printf ("%s",board_middle);
    printf ("%s",board_end);

    /* Print out a title. */
    printf (" * * *  M A S T E R M I N D  * * *");
}
```

This is slightly better than our first version. For example, if we wished to have a board edge made of ":" rather than "|", we only need then to change the "board_middle" string variable:

```
    char board_middle[]  = ":    |    :\n";
```

Chapter 10 - Other Arrays

We have seen how strings are declared - as an array of characters. We can declare arrays of other data types simply by *suffixing* the variable name with a number in square brackets:-

```
int card_values[4];
float stellar_magnitudes[10];
```

This declares an array of 4 integers and another of 10 floats.

The "card_values" array has 4 elements - card_values[0], card_values[1], card_values[2], card_values[3]. Assignment of an array element is achieved thus:-

```
card_values[3] = 10;
```

Here the [3] is said to be the **subscript** for the array reference.

Initialising Arrays

Arrays can be **initialised** as part of the declaration e.g.:-

```
int phaser_bank_levels[5] = {7,7,7,6,6};
```

to initialise elements individually   OR

```
int phaser_bank_levels[5] = {10};
```

to initialise all elements of the array "phaser_bank_levels" to 10.

10.1 Multidimensional Arrays

Can be declared by adding another index to the variable name:-

```
float daily_totals_by_week[52][7];
```

would declare a 52 x 7 array of floats, the 6th day 22nd week could then be referenced with

```
printf ("%f", daily_totals_by_week[21][5]);
```

10.2 Use Of Arrays

Arrays are commonly used to manipulate data as it would be in a table. Each "box" in the table corresponds to an *element* in the array. Consider the following example. Suppose we wished to store the rainfall (in mm) for a particular year. We would write it in a table:-

Jan	Feb	Mar	Apr	May	Jun	Jul	Aug	Sep	Oct	Nov	Dec
80	85	75	71	50	30	33	37	45	55	60	70

This could be stored in a 'C' program using the following array declaration.

```
int rainfall_in_month[12];
```

This could be extended to include initialisation thus:-

```
int rainfall_in_month[12] =
{
      80, 85, 75, 71, 50, 30, 33, 37, 45, 55, 60, 70
};
```

The array index figure, or *subscript* of 0 would be used to access the January figure, 1 would be used to access February, 2 to access the March figure and so on. Hence, if we wanted to print out the March figure, we would do:-

```
printf ("March figure for rainfall is %d\n", rainfall_in_month[2]);
```

As we shall see later, it is common to manipulate arrays in conjunction with "for" loops - we often wish to do the same thing to each item of data in the array (each element), so we have to use an iteration.

10.3 Codecracker Game – Storing our Secret Code and Guess

In our Codecracker Game, we will use **2 arrays** – one to store our secret code digits and one to store our guess digits thus:

```
char guess_digits[5];
char code_digits[5];
```

Later, we will write the code to read in the guess from the keyboard and also generate a secret using a random number generator function.

Chapter 11 - Keyboard Input

Most high level languages have a way of reading in data from the keyboard. In 'C', the way this is done is a little cryptic.

11.1 The 'C' Input Function "scanf" for reading strings and numbers.

The following 'C' program will read in a number and print it out.

```
int main( )
{
   int centigrade_value;

   printf ("Enter a value in Degrees Centigrade:");
   scanf ("%d", &centigrade_value);
   printf ("The value entered was %d C.\n", centigrade_value);
}
```

Notes
1. We first declare "centigrade_value".
2. We print out a prompt.
3. We read in the number from the keyboard.
4. We print out the value entered.
5. The "&" before "centigrade_value" is important - we will explain it later.

The 'C' function "scanf" is used to read in data from the keyboard. It is, more or less, the complimentary function to "printf". When "scanf" is used, it has at least 2 parts:-

```
scanf ("%d", &centigrade_value);
  (1)    (2)        (3)
```

The parts are:

1. Function name
2. Control String
3. Variable used to store the value read in

The control string *follows the same format as the one used for "printf" as described in section 8.1.* "scanf" can be used to read values into more than one variable at a time e.g.

```
scanf ("%c %d %f", &gender, &age_in_years, &weight);
```

Here, we have used "scanf" to read values into three separate variables "gender" (of type "char", "age_in_years" (an "int") and "weight" (a "float"). When these values are entered at the keyboard, they can be separated (in this example) by a space or spaces, or a carriage return.

We can use the control string to force values to be entered in a certain way e.g. to read in dates, separated by dashes:-

```
scanf ("%d-%d-%d", &day_number, &month_number, &year);
```

We can use this feature to check and validate inputs.

11.2 Single Character input – getchar() and getc()

Often, we just wish to read a single character from the keyboard (or somewhere else). We might want the user to press "Enter" after the character, or we might not. The getchar() and getc() functions allow us to do this.

For example, we could read single guess digits into an array with the following code:

```
char guess_digits[5];

guess_digits[0]=getchar();
guess_digits[1]=getchar();
guess_digits[2]=getchar();
guess_digits[3]=getchar();
```

An alternative way of doing this is to use **scanf()**, as discussed above. Hence we can now consider how another part of our Codecracker game will be written (though we will revise this later).

Note about the of a "getch()" function

In our final program, we will use a "getch()" function which will return a single character from the keyboard, without enter being pressed. This will make the final game a little more user friendly and it will make the input considerably easier to validate.

11.3 Codecracker Game – Reading in our Guess

We can now write a line of code to read in our guess.

```
char guess_digits[5];

scanf("%4c",guess_digits);
```

This would read 4 characters from the keyboard (the user would need to press enter, after the 4th character, though). The characters would be stored in the "guess_digits" array. However, there are 2 problems to consider:

What would happen if the user
- Did not enter numbers/digits but letters or other characters?
- Entered too few or too many digits?

Ideally, we need to "force" the user to only enter 4 **digits** (0 to 9) as anything else would not match our secret code. We will have to "cheat" slightly, here, in order to do this.

Chapter 12 - Decisions, Decisions...

Perhaps the most important feature of any computer program is its ability to make decisions - to do a conditional test. The way conditional tests are made in 'C' is similar to other high level languages.

12.1 Conditional Statements

There are a number of ways in 'C' to do conditional tests, but by far the most common is "if..else", which is shown below.

```
if (condition)
  one line statement;
else
  one line statement;
```

NOTE: Unlike some other programming languages, "THEN" is assumed and this word is not included in the "if" statement.

"if .. else" can also take a slightly different form using a "multi-line statement". This is shown below.

```
if (condition)
{
  statement 1;
  statement 2;
  .
  .
  statement n;
}
else
{
  statement 1;
  statement 2;
  .
  .
  statement n;
}
```

NOTE: Equality is tested for using "= =" e.g.

```
if (warp_factor == 10)
{
  printf ("The Engines can nae take it cap'n!!\n");
}
```

As with other languages, "inequalities" can be tested for. The following symbols can be used, where a "= =" ("double equals") might otherwise be used:-

Symbol	Meaning
!=	not equal to.
>	greater than.
>=	greater than or equal to.
<	less than.
<=	less than or equal to.

e.g.

```
if (i != 0)
{
    printf ("The number is non-zero.\n");
}
```

Another Example

Suppose we wished to check for a resistance value being greater than 1000 ohms, we could use the following conditional test.

```
if (resistance_value > 1000)
{
  printf ("Value is over 1 kilohm.\n");
}
```

To test for a number of conditions at once, the "AND" and "OR" keywords are required. In 'C', these are expressed thus:-

```
&&  - Logical AND.
||  - Logical OR.
```

e.g.

```
if ((character >= '0') && (character <= '9'))
{
  printf ("The character is a number. ");
}
```

Hints on Conditional Testing

A conditional test can be negated by placing a "!" in front of it e.g.

```
if (!((i >= 6) && (i <= 12)))
{
  printf ("Number is outside range 6 - 12");
}
```

Conditional tests can become quite complex. To keep them clear, it may be useful to follow these guidelines:-

- Each conditional test should be enclosed in (round) brackets.
- Try to stick to using the multi-line form of the conditional statement.
- Always align braces "{ }" which form the start and end of a block.
- If conditional tests become complicated, split them over a number of lines and align them sensibly.

12.2 More Complex Conditional Tests - The "switch..case" Statement

Consider the idea of writing a 'C' program to play a card game. Suppose you want to print out the card value in the form of its number, for cards 2 to 10, or A, J, Q, K for the others. If we assume an "int" called "card_value" contains a number in the range 1 to 13, we could do this in 'C' in the following way:-

```
if ((card_value >= 2) && (card_value <=10))
  printf ("%d", card_value);
else
  if (card_value == 1)
        printf ("A");
  else
        if (card_value == 11)
              printf ("J");
        else
              if (card_value == 12)
                    printf ("Q");
              else
                    if (card_value == 13)
                          printf ("K");
```

As we can see, this gives a somewhat large and unwieldy set of "if" statements. If we wished to do something as well as "printf" for each case, we would have to use the { } with each "if", making the whole thing more troublesome. Another way of doing the example would be...

The "*switch..case*" statement can be used to test a given variable for a number of discrete values. Other languages tend to use the "Case" statement alone. The previous example could be re-written thus:-

```
switch (card_value)
{       /* ↑ Control Variable */
  case 1:
        printf ("A");
        break;

  case 11:
        printf ("J");
        break;

  case 12:
        printf ("Q");
        break;

  case 13:
        printf ("K");
        break;

  default:
        printf ("%d", card_value);
        break;
}
```

Notes:

1. The "switch" statement takes the specified action for the specified value of the control variable.

2. After each action, the word "break;" is inserted to cause execution of instructions to carry on after the "}" of the "switch" statement. If the "break" is not included, execution continues into the next "case" action (which is occasionally useful).

3. The "default:" case specifies the action to be taken if the control variable's value is none of those listed in the other cases (this is optional).

4. Perhaps surprisingly, the statements in each "case" need not be included in { }. (Though any "if", "do...while", "for" statements contained in a "case" would follow the normal rules.)

Limitations of "switch..case"

- The control variable should be of type "int" or "char".
- The values being tested must be constants - i.e. you cannot use "switch" to test the value of one variable against another.

12.3 Codecracker Game – Some Conditional Tests

In our code cracker game, we need to do some tests.

1. Check whether we have had too many guesses.
2. Check whether the user wants to play again or finish the game.
3. Check whether the code the user entered matches any of the digits in the secret code.

The "checking against the secret code" step, we will leave till later, as there is a little more we need to learn before we can easily do this. For checking whether the user wants to continue the game we could do:

```c
char response;
response=getch();

if ((response=="y") || (response=="Y"))
{
  /*start a new game!*/
}
else
{
  /* exit from the game – end program!! */
}
```

But for checking the number of guesses, we can do:

```c
int guess_counter = 0;

/* Still things to do/think about here! */
guess_counter++;

/* We will allow 10 guesses
if (guess_counter > 10)
{
    printf ("You have lost!");
}
else
{
    /* Still things to do/think about here! */
}
```

We will see that our final code will be slightly different to this, but "we're getting there"!

Chapter 13 - Looping The Loop - Iteration

One of the things it is often necessary to do in a program is repeat something a number of times. We need to *iterate.* There are 2 main forms of iteration:-

1. Iterating a set number of times.
2. Iterating until a certain condition changes.

We can illustrate these forms as shown:-

1. Iterating a set number of times.

```
Initialise a count to minimum value.
Start
        Execute some instructions.
        Increase the count.
        Test if the count is greater than the maximum value.
                If No- Go To Start
                If Yes- Go To End
End
```

NOTE: The count could also be initialised to a maximum value and decreased to a minimum value.

2. Iteration until condition changes

```
Start
  Execute some Instructions (which affect the Condition).
  Test Condition.
  Is Condition True?
        No-Go To Start
        Yes-Go To End
End
```

> **NOTE: If the iteration is to be "finite" (i.e. finish at some point), the instructions which are executed must affect the condition in some way.**

Other Languages

Other programming languages have constructs for types (1) & (2) of iteration. Form (1) is expressed in BASIC as *FOR...NEXT.* In both BASIC and some other languages, (2) is in the form of the *REPEAT ... UNTIL* statement. We will now look at the 'C' equivalents.

13.1 Iteration Form (1) - The "for" Loop

It has this general form:-

```
     initialisation    continuation   iteration
         expr.            condition      expr.
           ↓                  ↓            ↓
    for ( i=0;            i < 10;         i++ )
       printf ("Spectrum is green!\n");
```

The action of the example is as follows:-

1. The "loop control variable", i, (which must be declared as any other data item) is set to zero.
2. The condition "i < 10" is tested, and evaluates to TRUE.
3. The "printf" is done.
4. i is incremented by 1.
5. Steps 2-4 are repeated until "i" reaches 10.

NOTE: The loop only continues to execute while the *Continuation Condition evaluates to TRUE.*

More Advanced "for" Loops

All parts of the "for" statement can have more than one part e.g. Assume i, j, k have been declared as "int":

```
    for (i=0, j=0;   (j<=9) || (k != 1); i+=2, j++)
    {
      <statements>
    }
```

In the above example, i & j are both initialised to zero, the Continuation Condition is evaluated (and is TRUE), the <statements> are executed, i is increased by 2 and j by 1. The loop terminates when j reaches 10, or when a 3rd variable, "k" gets set to 1 (happens somewhere in "<statements>").

NOTES:
1. With "for" statements, it is possible that the code inside the loop may never be executed (if the continuation condition always evaluates to FALSE).

2. All parts inside the ( ) of a "for" statement are *optional*, in other words this

```
    for (  ;      ;      )
    {

    }
```

is a legal piece of code - it represents an infinite loop (some times useful in "control" type programs).

13.2 Iteration Form (2) Do...While

This is very similar in form to the *REPEAT...UNTIL* statements used in BASIC and similar languages. e.g.

```
i=0;
do
{
  printf ("Spectrum is green!\n");
  i++;
}
while (i<10);
```

The action of the program is as follows:-

1. The "loop control variable", i, (which must be declared as any other data item) is set to zero.
2. The "printf" is done.
3. i is incremented by 1.
4. The condition "i < 10" is tested, and evaluates to TRUE.
5. Steps 2-4 are repeated until "i" reaches 10.

The only effective difference in operation to the "for" loop is that the condition is tested AFTER the action (rather than BEFORE).

MORE NOTES:

1. The code inside the "do" loop always executes at least once.
2. The main difference to *REPEAT..UNTIL* is that the condition tested is the *Continuation* condition (not the *Termination* condition).

Iteration Form (2) - "Reprise" - "While.."

There is a second form using "while", which is used in situations where you wish to test a condition BEFORE an action:-

```
    i = 0;
    while (i < 10)
    {
        printf ("Spectrum is green\n");
        i++;
    }
```

1. The "loop control variable", i, (which must be declared as any other data item) is set to zero.
2. The condition "i < 10" is tested, and evaluates to TRUE.
3. The "printf" is done.
4. i is incremented by 1.

5.   Steps 2-4 are repeated until "i" reaches 10.

> **NOTE: The action here is identical to that of the "for" loop, except we initialise "i" outside the loop. This form can be used wherever a "for" loop seems a bit Over-The-Top.**

Iteration Summary

As we have seen, there are three "looping" or "iteration" constructs in `C'. Examples are shown below

```
for (i = 0; i < 10; i++)
{
  <statements>
}
-----------------------------------------------
do
{
  <statements>
}
while (<condition TRUE>);
-----------------------------------------------
while (<condition TRUE>)
{
  <statements>
}
```

> **NOTE: Watch for the differing use of the semi-colon with the "while" statement.**

They are each quite flexible, and which one you use may depend on personal choice, although you should consider whether your iteration must be carried out at least once. (In which case choose "do..while").

13.3 Codecracker Game – Using Loops

We can now revise our earlier code to include a loop for each guess and also a loop for the whole game. It will look like this:

```
   /* Start a loop in which we will play the game. */
do
{
    /*Stuff will be added here later.*/

    /* Now loop for 10 guesses. */
    for (guess_no=1; guess_no <= MAX_GUESSES; guess_no++)
    {
        /* TO DO */
        /* Read in the guess - pass the current guess number. */
        /* TO DO */
        /* Mark the guess. */

        /* If we guessed correctly, break out of the "for" loop. */
        if (guess_correct == 1)
        {
            break;
        }
    }
    /* When we get to here, we will either have run out of goes, or
       "guess_correct" will have been set to 1 - the guess has been
       marked and found to be correct. */

    /* Check if we guessed it! */
    if (guess_correct == 1)
    {
        printf ("*** You Win! ***");
    }
    else
    {
        printf ("*** You have failed! ***");
    }


    /* Stuff to Add here!*/

    /* Now ask if the user wants another game. */
    printf ("Another Game (enter Y or N)?");

    response_entered = getch();

    /* Use "toupper" to convert it to upper case. */
    if (toupper(response_entered) == 'Y')
    {
        continue_game = 1;
    }
    else
    {
        continue_game = 0;
    }
}
while (continue_game == 1);
```

Note the use to "**toupper**" which converts the character to Upper Case, before we check it.

13.4 "break" AND "continue"

"break"

Can be used to break out of a loop when some condition occurs. Consider the following example:-

```
for (i = 0; i < 20; i++)
{
  if (array[i] == 0)
    break;
  array[i] = 1/array[i];
}
```

If an array element with a zero value is found, the for loop is terminated (the "break" is executed), and execution of the program continues at the end of the "for" loop.

"continue"

Causes control to pass to the end of the innermost enclosing while, do, or for statement, at which point the loop continuation condition is re-evaluated.

Example:

```
for (i = 0; i < 20; i++)
{
  if (array[i] == 0)
    continue;
  array[i] = 1/array[i];
}
```

If the array element had a value of 0, the division by 0 would *not* be done and the for loop would continue and processing of the next array element would take place. In other words, any statements following the "continue" are *skipped* and a return is made to the beginning of the loop.

Chapter 14 - Functions

Up until now, all the examples and programs we have looked at have been small and more or less self contained. One of the things about Computer Programs is that normally, they grow - and grow - and grow. If we always tried to do as we have done so far & write all our program between the { and } of "main", we would end up in a dreadful mess.

Initially, in considering the problem of writing a program, we said we had to break up the problem into smaller pieces. One of the ways we do this is to begin to use *subroutines*.

Subroutines

Almost all programming languages have ways of defining *subroutines* or *procedures* or *functions* - these are like small self-contained programs which we *call* from our "main" program. Subroutines would normally do one little job each - e.g. set up the screen or display a menu. For programs which are more than about 100 lines long, it is very important to try and consider how to break a program up into subroutines. This is called "structured programming".

In 'C', subroutines are called "functions". An example of how they are specified in 'C' is given below.

```
/* Define a function to print a line of stars. */
void stars()
{
    char some_stars[] = "**********";
    printf ("%s\n", some_stars);
}

/* Define a function to print a different line of stars. */
void edge_stars()
{
    printf ("*          *\n");
}

int main ()
{
    //A special command to Clear the console "screen" area
    printf("\033[2J");
    /* Call the "stars" function. */
    stars();

    /* Call the "edge_stars" function 3 times. */
    edge_stars();
    edge_stars();
    edge_stars();

    /* Call the "stars" function a 2nd time. */
    stars();
}
```

Program Notes

1. We define 2 functions called "stars" and "edge stars".

2. the functions just print out some asterisks.

3. We call the 2 functions repeatedly from the "main" program to produce the following output:-

```
* * * * * * * *        <-- stars
*              *        <-- edge_stars
*              *        <-- edge_stars
*              *        <-- edge_stars
* * * * * * * *        <-- stars
```

4. The function "stars" declares its own data - **this data cannot be accessed from "main"**. i.e. if we were to add the line

```
printf ("%s", some_stars);
```

anywhere inside "main", this would not work - *the program would not even compile. Why?*

14.1 Subroutines and "Local Data"

As we already mentioned, subroutines are like programs in their own right. As such, any data (variables) declared in a function *can not be used by other functions*, unless we take explicit action make this so.

Consider a room in your house, where you have some books on a shelf. If you go into another room, (and, say, close the door) you can not see those books. However, if you put your bookshelf, outside in the garden, you will probably be able to see it from both rooms, through the window.

We can do a similar thing with data in a 'C' program - we can declare it in a place where it can be seen by all functions. We do this by placing the data declaration outside all functions.

```c
char some_text[ ]="This can be accessed by all functions.";

void print_the_text( )
{
  printf ("Printing from the function...");
  printf (some_text);
}

int main ( )
{
  printf ("Printing from 'Main'");
  printf (some_text);
  print_the_text( );
}
```

Data declared in this way i.e. outside all functions, which can be accessed by all functions, is called *Global Data*.

14.2 Functions With Parameters

Passing Data to Functions

It is often common to pass data to procedures e.g. pass the value in degrees centigrade to a function and it prints out degrees Fahrenheit. The following example defines a new 'C' Function called "c_to_f" which takes a value in degrees centigrade and prints out a value in Fahrenheit.

type   parameter (also called *argument*)

```
/*
type        parameter type, parameter (argument)
  ↓              ↓            ↓
*/
void c_to_f (int         degrees_c)
{
  printf ("%d Degrees C = %d degrees F",
  degrees_c, ((degrees_c * 9) / 5) + 32);
}

int main ( )
{
  c_to_f (20);
  c_to_f (25);
}
```

Program Notes
1. We define a 'C' function of "type void" (see later).
2. We specify it will take single integer value as an *argument* or *parameter*.
3. We write the function so it just prints out the converted value.
4. We call the function twice from the main program, with slightly different values.

14.3 Returning a Value from a Function.

It is often very useful to pass some values to a function which then "processes" those values in some way and then *returns* a value to the main program. We can re-write the last program slightly to do this:-

```
return value type,        parameter type, parameter (argument)
    ↓                          ↓                    ↓
int c_to_f                (int            degrees_c)
{
  int degrees_f;

  degrees_f = ((degrees_c * 9) / 5) + 32;
  return (degrees_f);
}

int main( )
{
  printf ("%d degrees C = %d degrees f \n",
                  20,  c_to_f(20));

  printf ("%d degrees C = %d degrees f \n",
        25,  c_to_f(25));
}
```

Program Notes

1. The function is defined in the same way as the previous example *except* that it is defined to **return** a value to the main program.
2. The function is called twice from directly *within* the printf statement (Because we have defined the function to return a value, reference to it can be made in *exactly* the same places as a variable or constant, This is a very powerful feature of 'C' functions).

14.4 Using Functions

'C' Functions, then, fall into 2 main groups:

1. those which return values i.e. are defined to be of a certain *type.*
2. those which do not return values i.e. are defined to be of type **void** (no type).

You should therefore decide, when writing a function whether you wish it to return a value to the place from where it was called.

If you define a function *without* specifying any type at all (i.e. omit the "void"), the compiler assumes the function to be **of type int**.

14.5 Calling Functions Before They Have Been Defined.

Consider the following example:-

```
void function_a( )
{
  printf ("Function A, now calling function B...\n");
  function_b( );
}

void function_b( )
{
  printf ("Function B called.\n");
}

int main ( )
{
  function_a( );
}
```

In this example program, we are attempting to call function B from within function A. There is nothing wrong with this idea, but the example program will not compile. The reason is that when the compiler sees a call to function B in function A, it has no definition, so it assumes that B is a function of type "int". Later, it sees the definition for function B - and it is of type "void". This does not agree with the already assumed "int" type for function B, and so the compiler generates an error message. We can get around this problem as follows:-

```
void function_b(void); /* Pre-declaration or "Prototype" for  function B */

void function_a( )
{
  printf ("Function A, now calling function B...\n");
  function_b( );
}

void function_b( )
{
  printf ("Function B called.\n");
}

int main ( )
{
  function_a( );
}
```

This is exactly the same as the previous program, except that we have told the compiler function B will be of type "void". This is called a ***pre-declaration*** or ***prototype***. You could just put the whole definition of function B before function A, but this is not always convenient. **Function pre-declarations should also include the types of any parameters that the function uses:-**
We now change function_b to have an integer as a parameter:-

```
void function_b(int);/* Pre-declaration for function B */
/* B will take an "int" (integer)     parameter. */
void function_a( )
{
  printf ("Function A, now calling function B...\n");
  function_b(99);
}

void function_b(int any_number)
{
  printf ("Function B called with %d.\n", any_number);
}

int main( )
{
  function_a( );
}
```

The pre-declaration *must* agree with the real function declaration in **name, type and number and type of parameters.**

14.6 Codecracker Game - Functions Required

Now that we have learned about functions, we can re-consider the original flowchart and develop functions required to make our game work. This list should cover what we need!

```
/* Function pre-declarations. */
void draw_board(void);

void generate_code(void);

void read_in_guess(int guess_number);

void display_guess_on_board(int guess_number);

int mark_guess(int guess_number);
```

Values Passed as Parameters

- We don't to pass any values to "generate_code" or "draw_board" – they can do what they need without any additional information.

- We will pass the current guess number (count) to the "read_in_guess" function so that it can display a message to the user, telling them which guess they are currently on.

- We will pass the current guess number (count) to the "display_guess_on_board" function so that it "knows" how far down the board to put the guess.

- We will pass the current guess number (count) to the "mark_guess" function so that it "knows" how far down the board to put the marks.

Return Values

- The first 4 functions don't need to return any values passed.

- The "mark_guess" function will return a value telling us whether the guess was 100% correct, so that we know whether the game has ended and we can therefore tell the user.

Chapter 15 - Standard 'C' Functions

We have looked at how we can define our own functions, and pass "parameters" to them. One of the reasons why 'C' has become popular is because of what are called "Library Functions". There are thousands of library functions and they broadly fall into 3 main groups:-

- "Standard" C functions (ANSI).
- "UNIX" compatible functions.
- "System Dependant" functions.

There is some overlap between the first 2 groups. If you want to make your programs "portable" (i.e. compilable and runnable on different types of computers), you should use functions only from the first 2 groups.

We have already used several Library Functions - **printf, scanf, clrscr** and **getch.** These fall into another general group called "Input/Output" functions.

15.1 Header Files or ".h" Files

As we discussed in section 14.5, it is good 'C' practice to predeclare all functions that are used in your program – indeed, most compilers tend to enforce this practice by default. We have actually used some functions already - "printf", "scanf", "clrscr" and "getch". Strictly speaking, we should have pre-declared these functions in our programs before we called them. However, there is a short cut for doing this. For "printf" and "scanf" pre-declarations, we can add the following line to the very top of our program.

```
#include "stdio.h"
```

This line tells the compiler to "insert" the file "stdio.h" into the current file (but only during compilation). If you look in this file, you will find the pre-declarations for "printf" and "scanf", along with many other "Input and Output" (I/O) functions. That is why this file is called "stdio.h" it is short for "standard I/O" header file.

There are other header files which should be included when you use other pre-defined system functions. We will cover these as we come across them. You can define your own header files, for functions you define, but this is only really necessary when your 'C' program is split across a number of files.

15.2 Input Output Functions

- **printf** can take a variable number of parameters (not covered in this course). It returns no value.

- **scanf** can also take a variable number of parameters, and returns a value representing the number of input items matched and assigned.

- **getch** is a function which takes no parameters and waits for a key to be pressed. It returns a value representing the key pressed. (For letters and numbers this is the ASCII value of the letter or number.)

15.3 String Handling Functions

One of the most commonly used groups of library functions are the String Manipulation functions. When using string library functions in your 'C' program put the line

```
#include <string.h>
```

at the top of your listing.

Many standard 'C' functions (for historical reasons) have somewhat cryptic names. String handling functions are no exception.

Copy String Function - "strcpy"

In most other high level languages we can "copy" strings from one variable to another by simple assignment:-

```
First_string=Second_string
```

This would COPY all the characters from the variable "First_string" to the variable "Second_string".

If in 'C' we did the following:-

```
/* Declare 2 strings */

main ( )
{
  char text_string_1[ ] = "You are awful, but I like you";
  char text_string_2[ ] = "It's all done in the best POSSIBLE taste";

  text_string_1 = text_string_2;
}
```

This would not have the desired effect. Indeed, it may not even compile! This is one example of where C is revealed as a low level language.

String Copy Function - "strcpy"

To COPY characters from one string to another, we have to use a function; the 'C' function **strcpy**. The general form is:-

```
strcpy (<destination string>, <source string>);
```

In our example, we could do

```
strcpy (text_string_1, text_string_2);
```

The action of "strcpy" is to copy each character from "text_string_2" to "text_string_1" up until a "NULL" (0) character is reached - the end of the string.

WARNING: There MUST be enough space in the destination area to hold the string being copied e.g. make sure this **NEVER** happens:-

```
/* Any old string. */
char source_string[ ] = "Be careful using strcpy";

char destination_string[11] = "Too Small!";

/* Above is 10 characters + 1 NULL character." */
strcpy (destination_string, source_string);

/* This may cause your program to CRASH!*/
```

String copy "n" Characters - "strncpy"

This works in an identical way to string copy, but only copies the first "n" characters, or until a NULL character is encountered in the source string e.g.

```
strncpy (text_string_1, text_string_2, 10);
```

will copy the first 10 characters of test_string_2 to text_string_1 (or just text_string_1, if it is less than 10 characters long).

String Length - "strlen"

This function returns the length of the string as an integer e.g.

```
strlen ("Reeves & Mortimer");

would return a value of 17.
```

The value returned does not include the null i.e.

```
strlen ("\0");
```

String Compare - "strcmp"

This function compares 2 strings. It is used as follows:-

```
strcmp (string_1, string_2);
```

and returns 1 of 3 possible results:-

```
0 if the strings are IDENTICAL.

< 0 if string_1 is "alphabetically" less than string_2
> 0 if string_1 is "alphabetically" greater than string_2
```

Example call:-

```
char string_1[ ]="Only Me!", string_2[ ]="Only Me!";
.
.
if (!strcmp (string_1, string_2))
{
  printf ("The strings are identical");
}
.
.
```

(Of course, you wouldn't set up an assignment of 2 strings and then check if they were equal - one would normally be read from the keyboard and then you would use "strcmp" to check if the value entered was a certain string).

String Compare Ignoring Case "stricmp"

Same as "strcmp", but it ignores the case (upper or lower) of the characters in the string.

String Compare first "N" characters - "strncmp" & "strncmpi"

These are the same as "strcmp" and "stricmp", but only compare the first N characters:-

e.g. Compare the first 5 characters in 2 strings:-

```
char string_1[ ]="Poptastic, Mate!";
char string_2[ ]="Poptasticacious, Mate!";
.
.

if (!strncmp (string_1, string_2, 5))
{
  printf ("First 5 characters are the same.");
}
.
.
```

15.4 String to Number Conversion

To use these functions, put

```
#include <stdlib.h>
```

at the top of your file.

String to Integer Conversion Function - atoi

This function will convert an ASCII string of digits to an integer e.g.

```
int answer_to_l_u_e;

answer_to_l_u_e = atoi ("42");
```

String to Float Conversion Function - atoi

This function will convert an ASCII string of digits to a float e.g.

```
float body_temp;

body_temp = atof("98.4");
```

15.5 "Print" into a String - "sprintf"

"sprintf" is a very useful function. It can do all that "printf" can do, but it puts the result in a string. It is used in the following way:-

```
sprintf (destination_string, <control string>, parameters);
```

Want to convert a number to a string? Use "sprintf" .

15.6 Codecracker Game – Finishing The Program...

We have now covered or mentioned most or all the aspects of C that are used for our "Codecracker/Mastermind" game and you can find the finished program in Appendix 1 – Codecracker Program Listing. There are quite a few comments in the program and these should, when read after you have been through this guide, allow you to understand the operation of the program.

Chapter 16 - 'C' This Pointer - That's You, That Is

One of the things that is almost unavoidable when learning C is the use of pointers. Often, even the simplest program will use a pointer. This can make it much harder, initially, to understand what is happening, but hopefully, this next paragraph will help!

16.1 Computer Memory and Addressing

All digital computer memory is made of bytes (for the sake of argument, even modern computer memory which may only be accessed in 16, 32 or even 64 bit operations can just be considered as groups of 2,4 or 8 bytes). For the computer to access each byte (or word etc), there must be a mechanism within the system for identifying individual bytes of memory uniquely. This mechanism is known as *addressing*. It is a simple enough concept and the name is quite appropriate. On a street, each house is uniquely identified by its number, and the *address* of the house is the thing which is used to uniquely distinguish it from any other house on the planet.

Terrestrial Addresses can become quite messy and complicated and often have extra safety features "built in", such as a postal code, to assist or facilitate unique identification. With computer memory *each location is said to have a different address*. The address is normally a single number, written in decimal or, more commonly, hexadecimal format.

A computer's memory is normally viewed as a contiguous sequence of storage locations - each one being uniquely identified by its numeric address. The diagram represents a small block of memory where data can be stored.

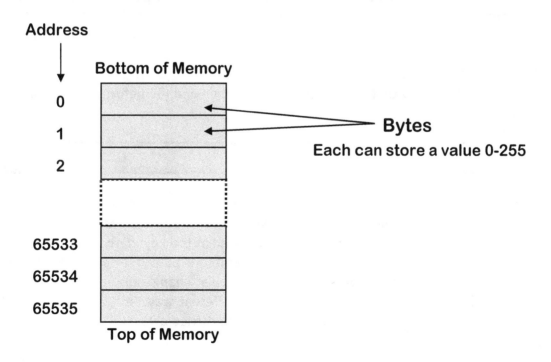

In the next diagram, we can see numbers being stored in a few of the boxes.

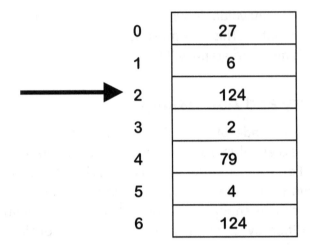

At address 2, the number 124 is stored. At address 4, the number 79 is stored. We can consider that the pointer is pointing to address number 2.

16.2 Pointers and Addressing

Essentially, you can consider that a pointer is just an address. In a C program, we can ask the system to tell us where our data is stored (as we shall below). We can then tell the system to do something to that stored data, by using the address (pointer). In simple terms, considering the diagrams above, if we wanted to change a value in one of the boxes, we would need to tell the system which box number we wanted to change.

16.3 That Weird Ampersand...

When we used **scanf**, we saw that we had to use the ampersand (&) before the variable name to get the desired effect e.g.

```
scanf ("%d", &centigrade_value);
```

to read a value into the integer variable **centigrade_value**. We have already discussed that scanf is a function. Here, it takes 2 parameters; the control string ("%d") and our variable. But, **scanf** needs to *change* the value of our variable to be the number entered at the keyboard in the execution of **scanf**. It is, in fact, *changing* the value of one of the parameters passed to it. In some programming languages, the declaration of the parameter you want to be a "changeable" one is specified differently – or you may find that you are forced to do things a different way. In 'C', you have to change the parameter declaration to use a ***pointer***. Before we get too carried away, let's do an example. Consider the following program:-

```
void print_the_number (int any_number)
{
  printf ("I was given the number %d to print!\n",
          any_number);
  any_number = 12;
  printf ("I have now changed the number to %d, so there!\n",any_number);
}

/* Program starts here. */
int main( )
{
  int a_number;

  a_number = 10;
  printf ("The value of the number is now %d\n",
          a_number);
  print_the_number(a_number);

  printf ("The value of the number is now %d\n",
          a_number);
}
```

Program Notes

1. Set up an integer variable with a value of 10.
2. Print out the value of this variable whilst in "main".
3. Call a function with the value as a parameter.
4. In the function, we print out the value again (it is still 10).
5. We then change its value to 12, and print it out once more.
6. Program execution then returns to **main**, and we print out our number once more.

The important thing to notice is that when we return to **main**, and print out our number for the last time, **it's value is still 10, even though it apparently got changed in the** *print_the_number* **function.** This is because *when we pass the number to the function,* **we pass a _copy of the value_ of the variable** *to the function, so the function can do what it likes to the copy of the value, and our original value remains intact and unchanged.* Hence, when we return to the **main** program, and print out our variable, the original value is seen. In this example the variable has been **passed to the function by value**.

It is quite common that functions need to be able to change variables used when they are not local - and also not global (as with "scanf"). The way this is done in 'C' is not quite as straightforward as in other languages, which are designed to remove the need to consider pointers as overtly as in C.

```
void print_the_number (int *any_number)
{
  printf ("I was given the number %d to print!\n",
          *any_number);
  *any_number = 12;
  printf ("I have now changed the number to %d, so there!\n",
          *any_number);
}

int main( )
{
  int a_number;

  a_number = 10;
  printf ("The value of the number is now %d\n",
          a_number);

  print_the_number(&a_number);

  printf ("The value of the number is now %d\n",
          a_number);
}
```

Without looking closely, there is not much difference to the previous example. However, there are some very important changes.

1. We have changed the way "print_the_number"'s parameter is declared. It has a "*" in front of it.
2. In the "print_the_number" function, we now refer to any_number as "*any_number".
3. In the main program, we have called "print_the_number" with "&a_number".

Doing all this means that within the function "print_the_number", we can change the value that is passed to the function. The value of the variable that is passed to the function is changed within the function, and the variable has the changed value *when it returns to the main program. Why?*

The reason is that we have passed the variable by **a pointer**.

16.4 Passing by Reference

In the diagrams above in section 16.1, we can also consider that each "box" holds the value of a variable in our program. By giving a function a pointer to a variable (i.e. the box number, not the actual value in the box), we can change the *contents* of that variable. You can actually use pointers anywhere in a 'C' program, not just in function parameters. Consider the following program.

```
int main( )
{
  int a_number;
  /* Declare a "pointer to an int". */
  int *a_number_ptr;
  /* Consider "ptr" to be an abbreviation for "pointer". */

  /* Set the pointer variable to point to the "a_number"
     variable. */
  a_number_ptr = &a_number;
  /* Initialise the variable. to 10. */
  a_number = 10;

  printf ("The value of the number is %d\n", a_number);

  *a_number_ptr = 12;

  printf ("The value of the number is %d\n", a_number);
  printf ("The value of the number (referenced through
          the pointer) is %d\n", *a_number_ptr);
}
```

Program Notes
1. We declare 2 variables; an "int" and a "pointer to an int".
2. Using the "&" operator, we get the <u>address</u> of the variable called "a_number" and store it in the pointer variable "any_number_ptr".
3. We assign "a_number" to be 10.
4. We print out the current value of "a_number" (10).
5. We change "whatever is pointed to by" (the "*" says this) a_number_ptr to 12.
6. We print out the number again twice. First we use the normal method, second we use a pointer reference ("whatever is pointed to by" again).

So, let's now try to describe the use of "*" (star) and "&" (ampersand).

& "converts" the object to a pointer - it gives the *address* of the object.

* when used in *data declaration* means "pointer to".

* when used in *assignment* means "object being pointed to by" - it "converts" the pointer to an object.

16.5 Pointers, Arrays and Strings

The way that 'C' handles arrays is closely linked to the use of pointers. It is common in some programs that pointer and array name references are interchanged. An array can actually be manipulated quite easily through use of a pointer.

The next program manipulates an array using a pointer.-

```
int main( )
{
  char character_array[10];
  char *character_ptr;
  char i;

  character_ptr = &character_array[0];
  for (i=0; i < 10; i++)
  {
        *character_ptr = i;
        character_ptr++;
  }
}
```

Program Notes

1. We declare a character array of 10 elements, a "character pointer" variable and a loop control variable "i".
2. We initialise the character pointer to the address of the first element of "character_array".
3. In the "for" loop, we set the "object pointed to by" character_ptr (an element of the array "character_array") to be the current value of the loop variable.
4. We increment the character pointer variable so that it points to the next character in the array.
5. We loop.
6. The only reason we haven't referred to "character_array" as a string is because it is not NULL - terminated - it does not have a zero character at the end.
7. The array elements end up with values from 0 to 9.

We could actually re-write the previous program slightly.

```
int main( )
{
  char character_array[10];
  char *character_ptr;
  char i;

  character_ptr = character_array;
  for (i=0; i < 10; i++)
  {
        *character_ptr++ = i;
  }
}
```

Program Notes

1. Here, we have initialised "character_ptr" using just the array name "character_array". If you refer to just **the array name**, it **means the address of the first element in the array** (whatever type it is). If you look back at our use of the "strcpy" (string copy) library function, this is actually what we were doing there.

2. We increment the character pointer in the assignment (this sort of thing is quite common in many programs).

16.6 More Advanced Pointer Usage

The next program implements its own version of the "strcpy" library function. It is a good example of how pointers are often used in 'C'.

```
void string_copy (char *destination_ptr, char *source_ptr)
{
  /* Just copy from source to destination until a NULL
  is reached - at which time the condition will fail! */
  do
  {
    *destination_ptr++ = *source_ptr;
  }
  while (*source_ptr++);
}

int main( )
{
  char source_string[ ] = "Reg Holsworth for PM!"
  char destination_string[50];

  string_copy (destination_string, source_string);
  printf ("My vote is ... %s\n", destination_string);
}
```

Program Notes

1.   We define a function "string_copy" which has two "character pointer" parameters ("char *").
2.   We start a "do" loop.
3.   We assign the character pointed to by the destination pointer to be the character pointed to by the source pointer, and (implicitly with the ++) increment the destination pointer.
4.   We test to see if what the source pointer is pointing to is a NULL (zero) character, and implicitly increment the source pointer. If we find a NULL character, it will be copied, but the loop will terminate.
5.   It is not generally recommended that library functions be re-written! This example is purely a demonstration of the way pointers can be used.
6.   This example illustrates the way in which quite a complex set of operations can be coded in a few short 'C' statements.
7.   The library "strcpy" function is actually of type pointer to "char". It returns a pointer to the destination string (in other words, the value of the first parameter).

> **NOTE: Great care should be taken when using pointers in 'C' programs. It is yet another area where 'C' assumes you know what you are doing. Incorrect pointer usage could result in loss of data or file corruption of any files your program is using.**

Chapter 17 - File Handling

One of the important features of programming languages is their ability to transfer data between the main memory of the host system and its disk storage e.g. say you had written a 'C' program to store results from an experiment, you would want the program to first allow the user to enter the values, then save them to a file on the disk. At a later stage, you then wish to retrieve this data into your program to use it for another purpose. Alternatively, you may wish to load the data into another package altogether - such as a Word Processor or Spreadsheet.

17.1 File Input and Output - File I/O

The general term applied to manipulating files from programs is "File I/O". In 'C' file I/O is done through the use of library functions, several of which are shown here:-

fopen (<filename>, <mode>)	Prepare file for use - returns value used for <stream>
feof (<stream>)	Check for end of file.
fprintf(<stream>, control string, variables)	Output stuff to file.
fputc (<stream>, char);	Output a single character to the file.
fgetc (<stream>);	Returns single character read from the file.
fscanf (<stream>, control string, variables)	Input (Read) stuff from file - like "scanf".
fclose (<stream>)	End use of file

There are a number of ways to do file I/O, not all of which will be shown here.

"fopen"

This is the function which, given 2 strings as parameters, will ask the system to prepare the file for use by your program and set things ready. The 2nd parameter to this function is a string indicating which "mode" you wish to access the file in:-

"fopen" modes

Mode String	Action/Description
r	Open for reading only
w	Create for writing. If a file by that name already exists, it will be overwritten.
a	Append; open for writing at end of file, or create for writing if the file does not exist.
r+	Open an existing file for update (reading and writing)
w+	Create a new file for update (reading and writing). If a file by that name already exists, it will be overwritten.
a+	Open for append; open for update at the end of the file, or create if the file does not exist.

For example,

```
fopen ("otis.txt", "wt+");
```

will attempt to open the file "otis.txt" in the current directory. If the file does not exist, it will be created. The program will attempt to open the file for writing, and in "text mode" (see later).

"fopen" returns a value which is called a *stream*. This is a special value which we use to access the file when we want to do fprintf, fscanf etc. It is like a "code number" for accessing the file (but it's actually a pointer to a block of memory about the file which the system allocates when it opens the file).

Relationship of File I/O to "Normal" (Console) I/O

Up to now, we have looked at how information is output to the screen (using "printf") and how we can read information from the keyboard (using "scanf"). One of the things about 'C' is that it attempts to treat all I/O in the same manner - in other words, outputting data to a file is very similar to outputting data to the screen. However, this is only true for ASCII files... read on.

17.2 ASCII File Output

This means file output which is "human readable" - i.e. the outputting of letters and numbers (and some special characters like Tabs, New Lines and Carriage Returns). This is done using "fprintf". It works in an exactly similar way to "printf" except that the printing is done *to the file* rather than to the screen.

```
#include <stdio.h>
int main(void)
{
    FILE *stream;
    int i = 100;
    char c = 'C';
    float f = 1.234;

    /* open a file for update */
    stream = fopen("otis.txt", "w+");

    /* write some data to the file */
    fprintf(stream, "%d %c %f", i, c, f);

    /* close the file */
    fclose(stream);
}
```

The action of the program is as follows:-
1. Declare a variable called "stream" to hold the "code number" (actually a pointer) used in accessing the file.
2. Declare an "int", "char" and "float" variable, and initialise them.
3. Open the file for writing and store the returned "code number" (pointer).

4. "Print" the values of the variables to the file whose "code number" is in the variable "stream".
5. "Close" the file.

Once this program has been run, you could, from the Command Line, do

```
pi@raspberrypi:~> cat otis.txt
```

and this would display the contents of the file which has been generated by the program:-

```
100 C 1.234
```

If you changed the "fprintf" statement to

```
fprintf(stream, "%d\n%c\n%f\n", i, c, f);
```

re-compiled and re-ran the program, you would see the following in the file "**otis.txt**"

```
100
C
1.234
```

17.3 ASCII File Input

It is possible to read data from a file as if it had been entered at the keyboard - this is achieved through the use of the function "fscanf" - this is a very similar function to "scanf" - it simply expects to get data from a file rather than the keyboard. Consider the following example:-

```
#include <stdio.h>
int main(void)
{
    FILE *stream;
    int i = 100;
    char c = 'C';
    float f = 1.234;

    /* open a file for reading */
    stream = fopen("otis.txt", "r");
    /* Check we have access to the file. */
    if (stream != NULL)
    {
        /*OK, Read some data from the file */
        fscanf(stream, "%d%c%f", &i, &c, &f);
    }

    /* close the file */
    fclose(stream);
}
```

The action of the program is as follows:-

1. Declare some variables - including one to hold the file "stream".
2. Attempt to open the file for reading from. If the file cannot be opened, "stream" will have a value of 0 (NULL).
3. Check if the file was opened correctly.
4. Read the three data items from the file and *into the variables* named i, c and f.
5. Close the file and finish.

The file would have to have data in it which matched what the fscanf was trying to read in hence, a file which contained

```
147 z 9.81
```

Or

```
147
z
9.81
```

would be OK (each thing separated by space or New Line). Once the fscanf in the program had executed, "i" would have a value 147, "c" would hold the character z and "f" would have the value 9.81. However, if the file contained

```
z
147
9.81
```

things would get "messed up," because the example "fscanf" was expecting to see a number first - what it actually saw was a character, so the variables would be set to the correct values.

17.4 Command Line Arguments

Consider the Linux command "cp", it could actually be written as a C program (as has been alluded to before when we were covering file / stream manipulation). The pseudo code for it might be as follows:-

```
   Check >2nd File< (destination) is not same as first. If it is, quit
immediately.
   Open >1st file< - "source" file.
   (***Someone missed out a line of pseudo code here)
   Open destination file.
   Repeat
         Read chunk of source file.
         Write chunk to destination file.
   Until (All source file has been read).
```

When we run the program the things marked like >this< are pieces of information which are on the Command Line. They are PARAMETERS to the copy command - the names of the files to be copied are supplied to the copy program as COMMAND LINE PARAMETERS. When the "copy" program runs, it takes the 2 strings supplied on the command line as being filenames. It then tries to open these files and actually do the copying.

(***The line of pseudo code which, years ago, was missed out in the original design of the cp command was the one which checks the destination drive / device to see if there is enough space to hold the destination file - if there isn't, the program should IMMEDIATELY quit.)

The command line arguments to copy are shown below:-

```
cp              mavis.txt       jack.txt
 ^argument [0]    ^argument[1]     ^argument[2]
```

In fact, most terminal commands - which are programs in their own right - take some form of command line argument.

Accessing Command Line Arguments from a C program

To access command line arguments from a C program is relatively straightforward. They are treated by a C program as a set of strings - an array. The following C program demonstrates this.

```
/*
     This is a program to demonstrate the use of command line arguments
*/
#include <iostream.h>
#include <conio.h>

// We modify the declaration of "main" so that we can access command line
//parameters...
/* The system organises them in the following way:-

        String              String Number
   +----------------+
   | Program Name   |        0
   +----------------+
   |                |        1
   +----------------+
   |                |        2
   +----------------+        .
   .                .        .
   .                .        .
   +----------------+        .
   |                |        no_of_strings (first parameter in
   +----------------+        declaration of "main" below).
*/
//Note, the use of the "char *" VERY important.
int main(int no_of_strings, char *command_line_strings[])
{
    int i;

    printf("\033[2J"); // A special command to Clear the console "screen" area

    //Print out the name of our test program - this is held as the
    //first string in the array:-
    printf ("The program executable filename is: \t");
    printf ("%s\n\n", mmand_line_strings[0]);

    if (no_of_strings > 1)
    {
        printf ("Command line arguments are:\n");

        //Now we print out each of the command line strings in turn.
        for (i = 1; i < no_of_strings; i++)
        {
            printf ("\t%s\n", command_line_strings[i]);
        }
    }
    else
    {
        printf ("No command line arguments given.\n");
    }
}
```

It is fairly simple to "bolt together" the things we used when accessing files to the above program to produce a new version of the linux "cat" command (which just displays files on the screen). The program for this is given below.

```
/*
    This is a program to demonstrate further use of command line arguments
    and is a simple version of the Linux/Unix "cat" command.
*/

#include <stdio.h>

// We modify the declaration of "main" so that we can access command line
//parameters...

int main(int no_of_strings, char *command_line_strings[])
{
    int i;
    char line_store[81];
    FILE *file_to_type;

    //Test the number of command line arguments which were supplied.
    if (no_of_strings > 1)
    {

        //Now we use each of the command line strings in turn:-
        for (i = 1; i < no_of_strings; i++)
        {

            printf ("Typing %s\t\n", command_line_strings[i]);

            /* Open the file. */
            file_to_type = fopen (command_line_strings[i],"r");
            //Check we were able to access it
            if (file_to_type == 0)
            {
              fprintf (stderr, "*** Couldn't open %s\n", command_line_strings[i]);
            }
            else
            {
                //Loop till the end of the file. */
                do
                {
                    //Read a single line of the file into our buffer.
                    fgets(line_store,80,file_to_type);

                    //Print the contents of the buffer on the screen!
                    printf ("%s",line_store);
                }
                while (!feof(file_to_type));
                // ^^^^ Continue until the end of the file is reached.

                //Close the file we have just read.
                fclose (file_to_type);
            }
        }
    }
    else
    {
        printf ("No command line arguments given.\n");
    }
}
```

As you can see, the above is a fairly short program - it will even type a number of files one after another - you just need to supply the names of the files you wish to type as command line parameters. If this were compiled into a file called "newcat", stored in the home folder, this can be achieved by:

```
pi@raspberrypi:~./newtype .profile .bash_history
```

this will show the contents of .profile .bash_history (2 files created by the system).

Note - it is common to see the use of the names "argc" and "argv" in the "main( )" declaration where "no_of_strings" and "command_line_strings" are used in the example above. The only reason they are called this is that whoever wrote the first 'C' program to access command line arguments referred to the parameters in the "main" declaration by these rather obscure names. Because "main" is a 'C' function like any other, we can give the parameters any name we like and make them as readable as possible. "argc" and "argv" probably (!) stand for "argument count" and "arguments vector".

Chapter 18 - 'C' Programming Style

Because 'C' is a "free format" language, it is quite easy to just "bash in" code without worrying about using a consistent or sensible layout, although most text editors of any sophistication have some kind of auto-formatting function, to help with layout. When writing programs, it is important to try and make them as readable as possible. This can be done by following simple guidelines:-

1.   Use sensible variable and function names with underscores for "spaces". e.g. use a name "centigrade_value" rather than "c" or "c_val". Or, if you do not like using the underscore, use capital letters in variable names e.g. "CentigradeValue". Remember that 'C' is case sensitive so get your capitals right!

2.   Space lines out well and indent sensibly e.g. put

```
if (centigrade_value == 30)
{
  printf ("Rather Warm");
  average_value += centigrade_value;
}
```

   rather than:

```
if (centigrade_value==30){printf("Rather warm");
average_value += centigrade_value;}
```

3.   Use comments liberally and sensibly and align them to the code they relate to e.g.

```
/* Read in the Centigrade value. */
scanf ("%d", &centigrade_value);
```

4.   At the top of each program (before anything else), put a comment box saying what the program does, and put in the date and name of the author. e.g.

```
/********************************************************
 *   File:                                             *
 *   Description:                                       *
 *                                                      *
 *   Author:                                            *
 *   Version:                                           *
 *   Date:                                              *
 *   History:                                           *
 ********************************************************/
```

5.   Before the start of each function, put a "block" comment describing what the function does e.g.

```
/****************************************************
 *    Function:                                     *
 *    Description:                                   *
 *    Parameters:                                    *
 *                                                  *
 *                                                  *
 *                                                  *
 *    Return value:                                 *
 *                                                  *
 ****************************************************/
```

Compare the styles of the following 2 'C' code listings and consider which is the more readable and why it is so (never mind what it does).

<u>Sample A</u>

```
while(1){
  x = 0;
  extchflag = EXTENDED_OFF;
  if( fpinmac ){
 fscanf(fpinmac,"%x %x",&extchflag,&x);
 if( (extchflag == 1 || extchflag == 2) && (x == KEY_RAT) ){
   fscanf(fpinmac,"%x %x",&ratx,&raty);
   clockwait(100);
 }else{
  timewait(1);
 }
  return(x);
  }

  if(ratpoint && ratflag){
 x = ratget();
 if( x == KEY_RAT){
   extchflag = EXTENDED_RAT;
   if( fpoutmac ){
    fprintf(fpoutmac,"%x %x",extchflag,x);
    fprintf(fpoutmac,"%x %x",ratx,raty);
   }
   return(x);
 }else if( x ){
   extchflag = EXTENDED_RAT;
   if( fpoutmac ){
    fprintf(fpoutmac,"%x %x",extchflag,x);
   }
   return(x);
   }
}
```

Sample B

```
/*********************************/
/*                               */
/*  Main Loop for all images     */
/*                               */
/*********************************/

/* Check we haven't already done this image. */
if (miniature_ptr)
{
  /* Set up some vars so we can use 'em easily. */
  working_image_width = page_image_width = miniature_ptr->original_width;
  working_image_height = page_image_height = miniature_ptr->original_height;
  page_image_x_coord = miniature_ptr->page_x_coord;
  page_image_y_coord = miniature_ptr->page_y_coord;
  x_page_offset_into_image = y_page_offset_into_image = 0;

  /* Invert the Y coord for use as an output page coordinate. */
  page_image_y_coord = (int)page_height - page_image_y_coord -
  working_image_height;

  /*********************************************/
  /* Check for image being partially off page. */
  /*********************************************/
  /* Check X */
  if (page_image_x_coord < 0)
  {
        working_image_width = page_image_width + page_image_x_coord;
        x_page_offset_into_image = page_image_x_coord;
  }

  if (page_image_x_coord + page_image_width > page_width)
  {
        working_image_width = page_width - page_image_x_coord;
  }

  /* Check Y */
  if (page_image_y_coord < 0)
  {
        working_image_height = page_image_height + page_image_y_coord;
        y_page_offset_into_image = page_image_height - working_image_height;
  }

  if (page_image_y_coord + working_image_height > page_height)
  {
        working_image_height = page_height - page_image_y_coord;
        y_page_offset_into_image = 0;
  }
}
```

Appendix 1 – Codecracker Program Listing

Here is the finished listing for the Mastermind Game. You will find a copy posted at http://chereprogramming.blogspot.co.uk/ or http://bit.ly/2pZLbOQ

As well as everything else, it is meant to be an example of good programming style. I therefore hope the comments in the code provide sufficient explanation of how the program works.

There are many ways to improve the program and many ways to code it. Remember, it has been presented as a learning exercise and is not meant to be the best, most complete or most optimised code listing. Additionally, it could be split into 2 or 3 modules. This "splitting" is one of the topics covered in the **Advanced C Programming guide**.

```c
/********************************************************************
 *      File:    masterrmind.c
 *      Date:    13.05.2017
 *      Author:  A.D. Johnson
 *      Version: 1.0
 *      Description:   Plays the game of "Mastermind." Uses (nearly all) standard
 *                     `C' so should be portable to other systems.
 *
 *******************************************************************/
/********************************************************************
This is a game where a sequence of numbers is set up - a "code" (normally by
a human, but we'll get the computer to do it), and the "codebreaker" tries to
guess the code as quickly as possible. He makes guesses by placing them on a
board. The "codesetter" then "marks" the guess according to certain rules:-

     If, in the guess, there is a certain number which is also in the code, but
it is in a DIFFERENT position, a WHITE peg is awarded.

     If, in the guess, there is a certain number which is also in the code, but
it is in the SAME position, a BLACK peg is awarded.

     Only 1 white or black peg per correct digit is awarded.

Example

     If the code was "1234" and the guess was  "4255", one black peg (for the "2")
and one white peg (for the "4") would be awarded.

 *******************************************************************/

#include <stdio.h>        /* Standard I/O - printf, scanf etc. */
#include <string.h>       /* strcpy, strcmp etc. */
#include <stdlib.h>       /* For rand() and srand(). */
#include <ctype.h>        /* For "toupper" - set to upper case.*/
#include <time.h>         /* For "time" function (used with "srand" below) */

#include <termios.h>      /* Linux System File */

/* Change this if you want more guesses in the game. */
#define MAX_GUESSES 10

/* Global data - the arrays used for the guess and code digits. */
char guess_digits[5];
char code_digits[5];

/* Function pre-declarations. */
void draw_board(void);
void generate_code(void);
void read_in_guess(int);
void display_guess_on_board(int);
```

```c
int mark_guess(int);

/********************************************************************
* Function:        gotoxy
* Parameters:      column - X, row - Y
* Description:     Moves printing position to specified screen/window location
*
* Returns:         Nothing
********************************************************************/
void gotoxy(int x, int y)
{
    // This uses what's called an ANSI escape sequence to move the cursor
    // to a particular location in the window.
    printf("\033[%d;%dH", y, x);
}


/********************************************************************
* Function:        clrscr
* Parameters:      none
* Description:     Clears the "screen" (console printing area)
*
* Returns:         Nothing
********************************************************************/
void clrscr()
{
    // This uses what's called an ANSI escape sequence to clear the
    // viewing portion of the terminal window.
    printf ("\033c");
}


/********************************************************************
* Function:        getch()
* Parameters:      none
* Description:     Waits for a single key to be pressed, rather than needing
*                  "Enter" or "Return" to be pressed - hence the jiggery pokery
* Returns:         The key code that was pressed.
********************************************************************/
char getch(void)
{
    int c=0;

    struct termios org_opts, new_opts;
    int res=0;
    //-----   store old IO settings in a structure -----------
    res=tcgetattr(fileno(stdin), &org_opts);

    //Keep a copy:
    new_opts = org_opts;

    //Update the bits we're interested in
    new_opts.c_lflag &= ~(ICANON | ECHO | ECHOE | ECHOK | ECHONL | ECHOPRT | ECHOKE |
ICRNL);

    //Put the settings into the system.
    tcsetattr(fileno(stdin), TCSANOW, &new_opts);
    //Check for a keypress
    c=getchar();
    //------   restore old settings ---------
    res=tcsetattr(fileno(stdin), TCSANOW, &org_opts);
    //assert(res==0);
    return(c);
}


/********************************************************************
* Function:        main
* Parameters:      none
* Description:     The main entry point to the program
* Returns:         Nothing.
********************************************************************/
```

```
int main()
{
    /* Data for "main". */
    int continue_game,guess_no, guess_correct;
    char response_entered;

    /* Start a loop in which we will play the game. */
    do
    {
        /* Clear the screen. */
        clrscr();
        /* Call the function to draw the board. */
        draw_board();

        /* Generate the code - in "code_digits". */
        generate_code();

        /* Now loop for 10 guesses. */
        for (guess_no=1; guess_no <= MAX_GUESSES; guess_no++)
        {
            /* Read in the guess - pass the current guess number. */
            read_in_guess(guess_no);

            /* Put the guess on the board. */
            display_guess_on_board(guess_no);

            /* Mark the guess. */
            guess_correct = mark_guess(guess_no);

            /* If we guessed correctly, break out of the "for" loop. */
            if (guess_correct == 1)
            {
                break;
            }
        }

        /* When we get to here, we will either have run out of goes, or
            "guess_correct" will have been set to 1 - the guess has been
            marked and found to be correct. */

        /* Move cursor ready to print out game result. */
        gotoxy(30,7);

        /* Check if we guessed it! */
        if (guess_correct == 1)
        {
            printf ("*** You Win! ***");
        }
        else
        {
            printf ("*** You have failed! ***");
        }

        gotoxy (30,9);
        /* Print out the code. */
        printf ("The code was %s...", code_digits);

        /* Now ask if the user wants another game. */
        printf ("Another Game (enter Y or N)?");

        response_entered = getch();

        /* Use "toupper" to convert it to upper case. */
        if (toupper(response_entered) == 'Y')
        {
            continue_game = 1;
        }
        else
        {
```

```
                continue_game = 0;
            }
        }
        while (continue_game == 1);

        /* Print out a closing message... */
        gotoxy (30,11);
        printf ("*** Bye bye... ***\n\n");
}

/******************************************************************
* Function:      draw_board
* Parameters:    none
* Description:   Draw a representation of the board in ASCII chars
* Returns:       Nothing.
******************************************************************/
void draw_board(void)
{
    int i;

    char board_end[]     = "+----+----+\n";
    char board_middle[]= "|    |    |\n";


    /* Set screen position to top left. */
    gotoxy(0,0);

    /* Print out the board. */
    printf ("%s",board_end);
    for (i=0; i < MAX_GUESSES; i++)
    {
        printf ("%s",board_middle);
    }
    printf ("%s",board_end);

    /* Print out a title. */
    gotoxy(30, 1);
    printf (" * * *  M A S T E R M I N D  * * *");
}

/******************************************************************
* Function:      generate_code
* Parameters:    none
* Description:   Put a random code into "code_digits" array of chars
* Returns:       Nothing.
******************************************************************/
void generate_code(void)
{
    int the_code;

    /* Set up the random number generator to give us a truly random value. */
    srand (time(NULL));

    /* Get a 4 digit random number. */
    the_code = rand() % 10000;

    /* Put this number into a string, in the right form. */
    sprintf (code_digits, "%04d", the_code);
}
/******************************************************************
* Function:      read_in_guess
* Parameters:    Guess number in game
* Description:   read in the guess from the keyboard.
* Returns:       Nothing.
******************************************************************/
void read_in_guess(int guess_no)
{
    int i;
    char key_entered;
```

```c
    /* Move cursor back to right place. */
    gotoxy(30,4);

    /* Print out a prompt. */
    printf ("Enter guess %d:      \b\b\b\b", guess_no);

    /* Read in 4 digits. */
    for (i=0; i < 4; i++)
    {
        do
        {
            /* Get the key pressed. */
            key_entered = getch();
        }
        /* Check the key pressed and loop if it's not valid. */
        while ((key_entered < '0') || (key_entered > '9'));
        /* Print out the key pressed. */
        printf ("%c", key_entered);

        /* Put the key in the guess array in the right place - "i". */

        guess_digits[i] = key_entered;
    }
    /* Set the end of "guess_digits" to be 0 - this is not really
       necessary, but we do it just to be sure. */
    guess_digits[4] = 0;
}
/*******************************************************************
* Function:      display_guess_on_board
* Parameters:    Guess number in game
* Description:   Display the entered guess in the correct place on board
* Returns:       Nothing.
*******************************************************************/
void display_guess_on_board(int guess_no)
{
    /* Move the cursor. */
    gotoxy (2, guess_no + 1);
    /* Print the guess. */
    printf ("%s", guess_digits);
}
/*******************************************************************
* Function:      mark_guess
* Parameters:    Guess number in game.
* Description:   mark the guess according to the rules and display result
                 on the board.
                 This is the most complicated function of the game but the
                 things we do in the function itself are quite simple.
                 We have to think carefully how we implement the rules of the
                 Black/white marking scheme, or we will not generate the correct
                 Results.

* Returns:       1 if the guess was correct (4 blacks).
*******************************************************************/
int mark_guess(int guess_no)
{
    char guess_copy[5], code_copy[5];
    int no_of_blacks, no_of_whites, i, j;

    /* Set the number of blacks and whites. */
    no_of_blacks = no_of_whites = 0;

    /* Make a copy of the guess and the code so we can muck about with them. */
    strcpy (guess_copy, guess_digits);
    strcpy (code_copy, code_digits);

    /* Do the blacks. */
    for (i = 0; i < 4; i++)
    {
```

```
                    /* Check if the corresponding digits of guess and code are the same. */
                    if (guess_copy[i] == code_copy[i])
                    {
                        /* Yes, so "knock out" this digit for when we come to do the whites. */
                        guess_copy[i] = '*';
                        code_copy[i] = '#';

                        /* Count the blacks. */
                        no_of_blacks ++;
                    }
                }

                /* Count the whites. */
                for (i = 0; i < 4; i++)
                {
                    /* We will compare each digit of the guess with each digit of the code. */
                    for (j = 0; j < 4; j++)
                    {
                        /* Here, we use the "i" loop for "guess", and the "j" for "code". */
                        if (guess_copy[i] == code_copy[j])
                        {
                            /* Make these digits in the guess and code copies "non-digits" so
                               that they don't get compared again. */
                            guess_copy[i] = '*';
                            code_copy[j] = '#';

                            /* Count the whites. */
                            no_of_whites ++;
                        }
                    }
                }

                /* Move print cursor to correct place on board display. */
                gotoxy (7, guess_no + 1);

                /* Print out the blacks. */
                for (i = 0; i < no_of_blacks; i++)
                {
                    printf ("%c", 'B');
                }

                /* Print out the whites. */
                for (i = 0; i < no_of_whites; i++)
                {
                    printf ("%c", 'W');
                }

                /* If we counted 4 blacks, we want to return 1, otherwise return 0. */
                if (no_of_blacks == 4)
                {
                    /* The code has been guessed. */
                    return (1);
                }
                else
                {
                    return (0);
                }
}
/*********************** THE END!!! ***************************
```

18.1 Possible Improvements to the Program

As mentioned above, there are many ways this program could be enhanced. For instance:-

1. Some of the 'C' code could be simplified in places e.g. when checking for a response at the end of a game.

2. The game could be made more "configurable" e.g. the user chooses how many digits there are to be in the code, and possibly selects a difficulty level which governs how many goes are allowed.

3. Colour graphics and sound could be used rather than dull ASCII characters.

4. A scoring feature could be added (and a high score table) with scores calculated on how quickly the code is guessed (and on difficulty). This information could be saved to a file.

5. The facility for another human to set the code for a friend (easy) could be added.

6. The code could be made much more difficult to guess by allowing letters to be used instead of numbers.

7. The game could be re-written to make the tea, do the washing up, hoovering etc :)

Appendix 2 - 'C' Here -Exercises

These exercises are given as some simple ideas for short programs to write, to get you practicing some of the techniques/ideas that you have learned.

So that you can use your solutions for future reference, when you save your "answers", under filenames with the appropriate question number e.g. save as "EX3.C" for Exercise 3 or whatever.

Printing Things

1. Write a program which prints

```
<your name>'s C Program! <Date>
```

   substituting in the appropriate information between the < > (chevrons).

2. Write a program prints "^^^^Whoosh!^^^^", followed by 15 "\n"s (new lines).

Variables and Initialisation

3. Write a program which declares 2 integers (int) called "zaphod" and "trillian", and uses a "printf" statement to print them out. What do you notice about the values of the numbers that are printed out?

4. Modify the program above so that the variables are initialised when they are declared.

5. Write a program which declares 2 floating point numbers (float) called "income" and "percent_tax_rate". Initialise them to 10,200 and 17.5 respectively. The program should then print out "The Tax Payable on " (income) "at " (percent_tax_rate) "is " (the answer).

Strings

6. Write a program which declares a string called "kryten" and initialises it to "Mechanoid 2000" and uses a "printf" to print it out.

7. Add to the program so that the 3rd character of the string and the 6th character of the string are printed separately from the rest of the string.

Reading in Numbers

8. Modify the program in Exercise 6 so that the values for "income" and "tax_rate" are read from the keyboard (scanf) with appropriate prompts.

9. Write a program which reads in a value in centigrade and converts the result to Fahrenheit, using the formula:

```
F = (C*9)/5 + 32
```

10. Modify the program such that it produces a more accurate result using floating point numbers (float).

Conditional Statements

11. Add conditional statements to the "centigrade to Fahrenheit" program such that when a temperature of 0⍰C or less is entered, the program reports "Whoa - freezing", when 10⍰C or less is entered, it reports "Bit chilly...", when 20⍰C exactly is entered, it reports "Ahhh - room temperature". When greater than 30⍰C is entered, it reports. "Ouch - boiling ot!".

12. Change the program such that when 20c if entered, it does centigrade to Fahrenheit conversion but if 68f is entered, it does Fahrenheit to centigrade conversion. (Hint: if you use a "scanf" with an "int" followed by a "char" variable, the variables will be set up automatically).

13. Write a program which reads in a number in the range 1 to 7 and then prints out the weekday. (Hint: use "if" statements to test the value of the number, then print out the appropriate day).

For Loops

14. Write a program which reads in 5 numbers, using a "for" loop, and calculates their average.

15. Modify the "average" program so that it first reads in the number of numbers (!) to be averaged.

16. Write a program which reads in four digits from the keyboard and stores them in a string called "guess_digits". Save this as "readgues.c"

Loops and Strings

17. Write a program which reads in a single word and says whether the letter "E" or "e" was entered. (Hint: You will need to use a loop to look at each character of the string. Remember to declare about 80 characters for your string so that it can hold a complete line of text. You can check for the end of the string by testing whether the character you are looking at is a '\0' or just 0.)

18. Write a program which reads in a string and counts the vowels in the string and prints out the number of vowels in the string.

The "switch" Statement

19. Write a program which prompts for and reads in 2 numbers. The numbers should be

    (i) a value of 1 to 13 to represent a card number (1 = Ace, 11 = Jack, 12 = Queen etc.).
    (ii) a value of 1 to 4 to represent a suit (1 = Clubs, 2 = Diamonds, 3 = Hearts, 4 = Spades).

20. The program should validate the numbers and print an appropriate message saying which, if any, is illegal. It should then print out a card name such as "Jack of Clubs" according to the numbers

entered. The program should use a "switch" case statement to printout the correct messages for the numbers entered.

21. Modify the program in 3 such that it prints out an entire list of all the cards in the pack (using a "do", "while", or "for" loop).

Functions

22. Write a program with a function called "print_total" which prints out the total of the 2 parameters passed to the function. You will need to pass 2 integer or float values.

23. Modify the program so that the function is called "calc_total" and it returns the total of the 2 numbers added.

24. Convert the program for calculating the Fahrenheit/Centigrade value to use a function – which takes centigrade as a parameter and returns the Fahrenheit value as a floating point value.

Pointers

25. Write a program which declares 3 integers "holly", "rimmer", "starbug" and initialises them 10, 20 and 30. Declare a pointer to an integer "integer_ptr". By setting the "integer_ptr" to point to each of "holly" and " rimmer" in turn, add the values of these 2 variables together through reference to the pointer and store the result in "Starbug".

26. Enter the function to copy one string to another (as in the notes). Change the function so that it returns a value indicating the number of characters copied. Add a "main" to the program and declare 2 string variables called "source_string" and "dest_string". Initialise the source_string to "vogon poetry" and call the function to print out the result of copying the string, and the function's return value.

Appendix 3 - 'C' QUICK REFERENCE

Main Program Form
```
int main ( )
{
  /* This is a comment! */
  printf ("Huh?");
}
```

All 'C' Statements end in ";" except before "{" (start of block). All **'C' reserved words are lower case**. 'C' is case sensitive.

Data Declaration
Always before code:-
```
int centigrade_value;       /* Integer */
long unemployment;          /* Large int. */
char any_char;              /* Character */
float exchange_rate;        /* Floating Point. */
char any_string[ ] = "Only Me!";   /* String */
```

Array:-

```
int card_values[52];        /* Array of 52 Elements. */
```

Array element references are numbered from zero e.g. card_values[4] is the 5th element of the card_values array.

Output To Screen - printf

```
printf ("The number was %d\n", centigrade_value);
```

Control String Elements

Conversion Chars.		Special Printing	
%d	integer	\n	New line
%c	character	\r	Carriage Return
%s	string	\b	Backspace
%ld	long	\t	Tab
%f	float/double		

```
printf ("%4d", centigrade_value);
```

specifies a field width (printing space) of 4. A "-" before the field width number means "left justify". "04" means print leading zeros. No. of conversion chars must match no. of following data items.

Input - scanf
```
scanf ("%d", &centigrade_value);
```

to read an integer into "centigrade_value". Conversion characters as for "printf".

Operators and Inequalities

```
tax = 10;       /* Assignment */
tax++;          /* Auto increment  +1 */
tax --;         /* Auto decrement - 1 */
tax += 20;      /* Equivalent to tax = tax + 20; */
tax -= 20;      /* Equivalent to tax = tax - 20; */
*               /* Multiply */
/               /* Divide */
%               /* MOD (remainder) */
i = = 10        /* Test if equal to */
i != 10         /* Not equal to */
i > 10          /* Greater than */
i < 10          /* Less than */
i > = 10        /* Greater than or equal to */
i < = 10        /* Less than or equal to*/
&&              /* Logical AND. */
| |             /* Logical OR. */
&               /* With 1 operand - address. */
*               /* Pointer to / object pointed to. */
>>              /* Shift bits right */
<<              /* Shift bits left. */
~               /* Bitwise NOT (1's complement) */
|               /* Bitwise OR. */
&               /* With 2 operands - bitwise AND. */
^               /* Bitwise exclusive OR. */
```

Conditional Statements
Simple statement:-
```
if (i == 10)
        printf ("Variable i is equal to 10");
```

Compound statement:-
```
if (i == 10)
{
        printf ("Variable i is equal to 10");
}
```

More than 1 condition:-
```
if ((i == 10) && (j == 11))
{
        printf ("Conditions Met!");
}
```

Conditions fail for a zero value and pass for a non-zero value.

Quick Reference 2
Looping

"for" Loop
Use an "int" for the variable below. Elements in "for" are initialization, continuation, iteration expression.

```
for (i = 1; i <= 4; i++)
{
        printf ("This appears 4 times!");
}
```

"while" Loop
```
i = 0;
while (i < 10)
{
        i++;
        printf ("i is now %d, i", i);
}
```

"do" Loop
```
i=0;
do
{
        i++;
        printf ("i is now %d, i", i);
}
while (i < 10);
```

Code always executes at least once.

"switch" statement
Use integer for control variable:-

```
switch (card_value)
{
  case 1:
        printf ("Ace");
        break;
  case 11:
        printf ("Jack");
        break;
  .
  .
  default:
        printf ("%d", card_value);
}
```

Functions
```
/* 3 functions will be declared below. */
int global_integer;   /* Global data declared outside*/
                    /* all functions. */
void function_b(void);  /* Predecl. for function_b */

void function_a(int any_number) /* returns nothing*/
{   /* takes integer ^^ parameter */
        /* Integer only used in this function. */
        int local_integer;
        printf ("The number is %d", any_number);
}

int function_c (int any_number) /* returns an integer*/
{           /* ^^ takes integer parameter */
  function_b( );   /* Call "function b" */
  printf ("The number is %d", any_number);
  /* Just add 10 and return the value. */
  any_number += 10;
  return (any_number);
}
/* Function which has no parameters and no return
value.*/
void function_b ( )
{
    printf ("This is function b! ");
}

int main ( )
{
    /* Call function a. */
    function_a(10);
    /* Call function c. */
    function_c( );
}
```

Library Functions
At top of program put:-

```
#include "stdio.h"        /*For printf, scanf etc. */
#include "string.h"       /*For string functions. */
#include "stdlib.h"       /*For standard 'C' library */
```

String Functions

strlen (string);	String length
strcpy (dest, source)	String copy
strncpy (dest, source, number)	Copy n characters
strcmp (string1, string2)	String compare (returns 0 if equal)
strncmp (string1, string2, n)	String compare 1st n
stricmp (string1, string2)	Compare without case
strncmpi (string1, string2)	Comp 1st n - no case
sprintf (string, control sting, etc)	"printf" into a string.
centigrade_value = atoi (string)	Convert string to int

Standard 'C' Library

srand (long)	Set seed for "rand".
rand ( )	returns random value 0-65535.